Fashion. A Theory.

FREDERIC MONNEYRON

FASHION. A THEORY

© 2024 OpenCulture Academic Press
Edition and layout : Reedsy
Find our catalog at http://openculture.fr/
Contact : infos@culturea.fr

ISBN paperback : 9791043111778

ISBN hardback : 9791043111761

ISBN e-book : 9791041989973

Legal deposit : December 2024

All rights reserved

This book supports Plantons Pour l'Avenir, an endowment fund
for the reforestation of French forests - more than
400 forest reforestation projects supported since 2014 across
France https:/ / www.plantonspourlavenir.fr/

CONTENTS

PREFACE

Dear readers,

It is with great pleasure that I present to you this remarkable work, *Fashion: A Theory*, the result of Frederic Monneyron's passionate and rigorous efforts. As a sociologist specializing in the study of cultural phenomena and creative industries, I had the honor of following the evolution of this project until its completion in book form.

The structure of the book reflects Frédéric Monneyron's desire to offer a unified theory of fashion by articulating different disciplinary perspectives. The book opens with a first part entitled "Clothes and Societies", which explores the links between clothing and social anticipation. Monneyron highlights the importance of designers and fashion magazines in the construction of trends and sartorial imaginaries.

The second part, "Fashion Images and Social Figures", delves into the spatio-temporal dimension of fashion, as well as its relationship to sexual identities and sexuality. The author shows how fashion participates in the construction of social representations and gender norms while offering spaces for subversion and creativity.

The chapter devoted to "Societies" is particularly enlightening. Monneyron analyzes how fashion reflects and shapes social dynamics by playing on the logics of distinction, imitation, and diffusion. He draws on numerous concrete examples, ranging from the dress codes of urban subcultures to the positioning strategies of major luxury houses.

The third part of the book, "Three Designers", offers a fascinating dive into the world of three iconic French designers: Yves Saint Laurent, Jean-Paul Gaultier, and Christian Lacroix. Through these case studies, Monneyron highlights the connections between individual creation, socio-historical context, and collective imaginaries. The analysis of Yves Saint Laurent's work in the 1970s is particularly striking. Monneyron shows how the designer captured the spirit of an era marked by women's liberation movements and cultural revolutions while reinventing the codes of French elegance. The chapter on Jean-Paul Gaultier explores the subversive and ironic dimension of his work in relation to the social and cultural changes of the 1990s. Monneyron finely analyzes how Gaultier plays with gender stereotypes and marginal identities while establishing himself as a major figure in contemporary fashion.

Finally, the study devoted to Christian Lacroix highlights the uniqueness of this designer, who managed to assert himself "against the grain" of dominant trends. Monneyron shows how Lacroix draws on Provençal sartorial traditions and decorative arts to create a baroque and flamboyant universe, going against the minimalism in vogue in the 1980s and 1990s.

Throughout these analyses, Frederic Monneyron skillfully brings together the tools of sociology, history, and semiology to decipher the deep springs of fashion creation. His approach, which in some respects echoes Gilbert Durand's work on the anthropological structures of the imaginary, offers a particularly fruitful framework for understanding fashion as a total social fact. Gilbert Durand was a major thinker who theorized a rehabilitation of the imaginary, long devalued by Western thought. In his seminal work *The Anthropological Structures of the Imaginary* (1960), he develops a figurative structuralism highlighting three major symbolic structures (heroic, mystical, and synthetic) that organize the productions of the imaginary. His multidisciplinary approach, combining philosophy, the study of myths, history of religions, depth psychology, and anthropology, paved the way for a genuine anthropology of the imaginary. However, while Durand's influence has been considerable in France and Europe, his reception in the United States has remained more limited. American sociology has developed more in a rationalist and positivist perspective, giving less space to the symbolic and imaginary dimensions of the social.

In this context, Frederic Monneyron's book "Fashion: A Theory" appears as an important contribution to making the sociology of the imaginary known and legitimizing it across the Atlantic. By applying a Durandian approach to the analysis of fashion, Monneyron shows the fruitfulness of this current to illuminate a total social fact. Through his case studies on Yves Saint Laurent, Jean-Paul Gaultier, and Christian Lacroix, he highlights how fashion designers mobilize and reconfigure the major anthropological structures of the imaginary identified by Durand. Monneyron thus shows how fashion, far from being reduced to a superficial phenomenon, is rooted in the collective imaginary and in turn helps to shape it. As he recognises himself : "Accordingly, clothing should be regarded not only as being part of the anthropological objects of Gilbert Durand's mythoanalysis but also as a fundamental element of it".

More broadly, *Fashion: A Theory* illustrates the relevance of the sociology of the imaginary for analyzing a multitude of fields of contemporary sociality, from the most classic to the most novel. By placing *homo imaginans* at the heart of sociological reflection, it opens up new perspectives to enrich our understanding of the social.

Ultimately, through its theoretical ambition and the richness of its empirical analyses, Monneyron's book appears as a major contribution to making the sociology of the imaginary known to the American public. It demonstrates the fruitfulness of this current to renew the sociological gaze by rehabilitating the place of images, symbols, and myths in the construction of social reality.

Let us hope that *Fashion: A Theory* will spark new debates and open up new avenues of research on Fashion at the intersection of the social sciences and humanities.

Frédéric Gimello-Mesplomb

FOREWORD

Clothes are truly subject to a peculiar neglect. While they clearly set humans apart from animals, differentiate individuals instantly, and mark specific eras, they have rarely been thoroughly examined. Their role in shaping both personal and social identities is often overlooked; their importance in social integration or dissent is underappreciated; and their influence on social behavior isn't sufficiently recognized. For instance, the way we dress for a formal event, a garden party, or a tennis match affects how we behave in those settings. The mundane nature of clothes might be the main reason they're not studied or discussed much. This seemingly trivial point shouldn't be dismissed outright, yet their perceived frivolity may also contribute to their exclusion from serious research. In Western societies, a long-standing philosophical tradition prioritizes deeper meanings over surface appearances, thus reducing clothes to mere false impressions, favoring an unvarnished truth instead.

Then, to write on clothes implies the reversal of a whole philosophical attitude: trying no more to pose clothes as a source of mistakes, but as a mold, matrix, no longer as a secondary and accessory element, but as a very first and founding element, determining individual behaviors as the social structures. It is this reversal that, in a large interdisciplinary perspective, the conference I organized at Cerisy in July 1998 has already tried to promote. The conference has set the very basis and directions for further research. But this book tries to address what is obviously missing: a theory, and also —theories being reinforced by practices— the sociological practices of clothes and fashion. For failing to carry on the necessary reversal, the few attempts that have been made to date, from Quentin Bell's and James Laver's books.[1] to the *Système de la mode*, Roland Barthes's semiological opus, passing through more recent feminist studies, did not succeed in putting forth a very convincing perspective.

Some other considerations pushed me in that direction, too. An impression first: the impression that Norbert Elias, in his well-known analysis of the slow psycho-social integration of all the constraints that have modified our behavior and contributed to the "dynamics of the Western world" has forgotten, or at least underestimated, the part played by clothes. A regret, too. In the wake of my own research on the androgyne and on seduction,[2] in contexts where clothing was already an important element, I regret not giving it an even more significant role in the

---

1. Q. Bell, *On Human Finery*, London: 1976; R. König, *Kleider und Leute, Zur Soziologie der Mode*, 1968.

2. See F. Monneyron, *L'Androgyne décadent. Mythe, figure, fantasmes*, Grenoble: Ellug, 1996 and *Séduire, L'Imaginaire de la séduction de Don Giovanni à Mick Jagger*, Paris: PUF, 1997 and Imago, 2016.

construction of sexual identities. Following these considerations, here are the questions that guided me: How can wearing a particular dress modify behavior or determine an identity? More generally, what is the social function of fashion today, and if it fundamentally provides models, how does it do so? Indeed, these models stem from images inspired by clothes. To what extent, then, are these fashion images, which have rarely been studied as such, significant indicators of a society's state? Additionally, what is elegance? Beyond the vicissitudes of fashion and time, does elegance exist *in itself*? If there are only different ways of being elegant, how can we define them?

To answer these questions and the ones that they stimulate, I have smoothly organized this essay in which the theory is followed by the analysis of an important iconography. The study of global clothing creation in a society is combined with the study of individual creations. However, some of these directions call for more comments.

When it came to applying the theoretical directions I have defined above, in other words, analyzing fashion images, I focused on the last fifty years that show some unity as they begin with the birth of ready-to-wear. It is more convenient, undoubtedly, to garner a consistent and significant iconography for a recent period than for a past one, but in doing so, I did not go for the easy option; I tried to deal with a significant concern. I was not intent on questioning the historical approach: it is, in many respects, indispensable and has produced the most exciting and innovative books on the subject,[3] but I did challenge the historicism of the books dealing with clothing and fashion, the best and the worst, that don't pave the way to a deeper hermeneutics. To set the time period to study, in part or in totality, in the lifetime of most of the readers and provide them with the necessary references and the possibility to relate to their own experience was also a way to measure and assure the validity of this hermeneutics.

Another concern arose when I focused on individual designers and attempted to link their work to a specific period without aiming to be exhaustive. Instead of expanding the research, it was preferable to focus on three highly illustrative creators. Indeed, others would have warranted a similar study where their creativity is analyzed as a writer's would be. However, in the decision I made to examine Yves Saint Laurent —whom Marguerite Duras could only perceive as a writer—[4] Jean-Paul Gaultier and Christian Lacroix, I have pointed out the relations of three individuals to their time, as well as to elegance.

At last, for the analysis of fashion images to be larger than a mere and superficial description —a level that in many works it doesn't go beyond— it had to be grounded in a hermeneutics of images set on a more

---

3. Ph. Perrot, *Les Dessus et les dessous de la bourgeoisie. Une histoire du vêtement au XIXe siècle*, Paris: Fayard, 1981 and D. Roche, *La Culture des apparences. Une histoire du vêtement (XVIIe-XVIIIe siècle)*, Paris: Fayard, 1989.

4. M. Duras, *Le Monde extérieur*, Paris: P.O.L., 1993, p. 165.

significant philosophical vision. There is little doubt that this hermeneutics could not be found but in Gilbert Durand's anthropology, the only one to offer a perspective that conjugates depth and epistemological coherence. And, that is, indeed, in adapting, with some methodological imagination, the main principles of the *Anthropological Structures of the Imaginary* to the very objects of clothing and fashion, that this book has achieved its best results and revealed what the stakes and the sense of appearance are.

I.   CLOTHES AND SOCIETIES

CHAPTER 1

CLOTHING AND SOCIAL ANTICIPATION

If you agree with the widely held belief that fashion is a never-ending cycle, existing only to cease existing, then you might also find it plausible, as some historians do, that clothing has undergone its own unique evolution.

But, this very idea is more or less acceptable. It depends on the way it is interpreted. If "an evolution of one's own" means that clothing has no relation whatsoever with history, one may be reluctant, indeed, to accept it. In opposition, if it means that clothing doesn't depend directly on history, i.e. that clothing is not only the superficial manifestation of more profound changes but is something much more complicated, then this idea is far more acceptable. Anyway, that is what I would like to elaborate on.

I would like to show that clothing doesn't follow history but to a large extent (and it is somehow provocative) that clothing always comes first, in other words, that clothing makes history. Let's make it clear: that much of our ways of behaving (the way we walk, the way we move) are determined by it[5] ... that any

---

5. See G. Simmel, *Philosophie de la modernité*, Paris: Payot, 1989.

important social change begins with this shallow activity that we call "parler chiffons", to talk clothes.

Firstly, one should find some anthropological argument for this. One can stress the fact that the very act of getting dressed, because it distinguishes man from animal as Condorcet used to say, has a foundational aspect. This is also because it emerges, like sexuality and food, as a fundamental activity of the human being, decisive in every process of socialization,[6] that, consequently, by no means can be rationalized and partakes of symbolism and imaginary. As a good example of it, without even calling in Baudelaire stressing on "the high spirituality of clothes" that "those our confused and perverted civilization calls savages (...) understand as well as the children",[7] we can underline that in traditional societies, symbolic values and functional values of clothes are linked together. All traditions agree to see in the pleat of handmade fabrics an image of the first sun ray at the dawn of creation and in their sewing the representation of plans of being or of levels of references, more or less far apart, but depending on their common center and on their first support.[8] Accordingly, clothing should be regarded not only as being part of the anthropological objects of Gilbert Durand's mythoanalysis but also as a fundamental element of it. Besides, if we consider, with

---

6. See Cl. Lévi-Strauss, *L'Homme nu*, Paris: Plon, 1971.

7. Ch. Baudelaire, *Oeuvres Completes*, Paris: Gallimard, 1975.

8. See A.K. Coomaraswamy, *The Christian and Oriental Philosophy of Art*, New York: Dover Publications Inc.,1956.

Gilbert Durand, that history is not the pattern of the myth but that the myth is the pattern of history,[9] in other words, if the myth is at the origin of historical thought, then we may also consider that the importance of clothing in history itself is far greater than we may think.

However, to find the priority of clothing, we must fight against a whole philosophical tradition. The Western way of thinking has tried to find the soul under the body (in religious terms), the superstructure under the economic infrastructure (that was the Marxist point of view, but that is also the credo of liberalism), under the conscious way of being and speaking the Unconscious (in psychoanalytic terms). And, more generally, the Western philosophical tradition has tried to find the Being under appearance and has pointed out that "L'habit ne fait pas le moine," that clothes do not make the man.

Therefore, in opposition to those who think that the appearance could not stand for the Being, it is quite possible to reconsider the proverb with Jacques Lacan but also, before him, with Thomas Carlyle, and not to see clothing as something shallow but as a social pattern that determines the way of being and living, and consequently, in fashion, a good approach to all social trends.

At the end of the nineteenth century, Oscar Wilde, in *The Decay of Lying,* focused on the fact that "Life imitates art far more than art imitates life". And

---

9. G. Durand, *Figures mythiques et visages de l'oeuvre*, Paris: Berg International, 1979, p. 306.

we may say, after him, that the very function of art is not, indeed, to imitate nature as Aristotle defined it, but also to create patterns that will inform reality and give structures to society.

Indeed, the internal connections of art, as well as the theoretical frameworks developed by some artists and quickly assimilated by some witnesses in their personal experiences, are its primary characteristics. In other words, art creates patterns that will be imitated by a large amount of people in their own life. But art can only be a model to our experiences, if art firstly changes our structures of perception. In other words, it is in changing the way we see things, that art can change our social behaviours. However, this particular art form which is fashion, Baudelaire regarded as "a sublime deformation of nature or rather as a permanent and successive effort of reformation of nature,"[10] doesn't need to change our structures of perception, for it concerns, before everything else, the body; doesn't exist but on the body. Accordingly, fashion creates patterns much more directly, but also much more securely than any other form of art.

These patterns created by the designers are to be socially imitated. Imitation has been interpreted as a social concept at the end of the nineteenth century. The great French sociologist Gabriel de Tarde sees imitation, in *The Laws of Imitation,* his main work, as the very principe of human activity and sees society as an ensemble of individuals imitating each other. He insists

---

10. Ch. Baudelaire, «Eloge du maquillage», *Oeuvres complètes,* Paris: Gallimard-Pléiade, p. 1184.

on the fact that the individuals *regarded* as superior, in general or in a given field of activity, are imitated by the others in general or in that given field of activity.[11] This imitation applies obviously to clothing, which partakes of these needs of luxury that are taking over primitive needs.[12] Another author has pointed it out clearly : Thorstein Veblen. In his well-known book, *Theory of the Leisure Class*, he considers that in modern clothing, the adornment is taking over the need to cover the human body. And he underlines that if, in most cases, the conscious motivation of a man who gets dressed or buys expensive clothes is the need to be in line with the established practice and with the model of taste, this man also obeys the exigencies of expensiveness, for, among our ideas on clothes, is the idea that all the clothes that don't cost a high price are ugly. Besides, he explains that elegant clothes have an effect because they cost a high price and because they are an attribute of leisure. The ones who wear them show they can consume an important amount of richness, but that they can consume it without having to work.[13]

Whatever our conception of imitation may be, this imitation process goes through a certain number of mediators which help to build up a pattern and, accordingly, to stimulate a social evolution. No doubt that fashion magazines, on which I shall come back to in chapter 2, have had this function for quite a long

---

11. G. de Tarde, *Les lois de l'imitation, étude sociologique* (1899), Paris: Kimé, 1993, p. 252.

12. *Ibid.,* p. 213.

13. Th. Veblen, *Theory of the Leisure Class* (1895), New York: Dover Publications Inc, 1994.

time, but the fashion model, this quite modern institution, is still a better example.

We may say that fashion as an art form asks for a schema for every individual, but this problem is partly resolved thanks to the fashion model. The fashion model is the embodiment, to many women, of their ideal; the model is an embodied idea that is, in turn, multiplied by photography. Some designers have insisted on this mediation of the model. Yves Saint Laurent, for instance, used to say: "Fashion models? They are only models. I don't think of them as women. If I may be attracted by one of them, that is only to show out a line."[14] This function of fashion to create patterns that, once imitated, decide what our representations will be, dictate our ways of being, and anticipate changes, exerts on the main structures of our societies. Clothing anticipates the coming state of society, just as those logical "models" used for economic and political forecasts. For instance, we may very well regard the uniformization of clothes in 19th-century France not only as the result of social changes: the end of the privileges of the aristocracy and the clergy and the coming of the age of the bourgeoisie but also as the very principle of further democratic aspirations, which are the hallmark of the century. In other words, as there are only a few differences left in the way of getting dressed, one wants to suppress the differences between individuals. The uniformization of clothing anticipates a new reduction of social

---

14. See L. Benaïm, *Yves Saint Laurent*, Paris: Grasset, 1993, p. 122.

differences as well as a quest for individualism, which is not contradictory.[15] From the nineteenth century on, clothes speak less and less of social taste and more and more of individual taste; they indicate the personality of an individual rather than a social group or rank. A similar analysis can be made for the new stage in the uniformization of clothing, fostered more recently - actually in the 1960s - by the ready-to-wear that, after popularizing the Parisian Haute Couture creations (especially in the United States), dressed very soon, whatever are its variations: luxury or high street fashion, most of the inhabitants of the developed countries, from the billionaires to the lower classes, such that the social differences in the way of getting dressed are no more significant.[16] Far from only being one of the many effects of a consumer society that reduces economic and social differences, this new uniformization is to be regarded as expressing in advance even more extraordinary exigencies for democracy and liberty. In this regard, a piece of clothing like *jeans*, with their large consumption in the Western world being contemporary to ready-to-wear, provides a good example. Initially, American working-class clothing was quickly forgotten and their triumph and hegemony didn't mean the triumph and hegemony of the working class. However, to the youth at first, then to a more significant part of the wearers, they are the symbol of rebellion and

---

15. See L. Dumont, *Essais sur l'individualisme*, Paris: Seuil, 1983 and *Homo Aequalis I* and *II*, Paris: Gallimard, 1985 and 1992.

16. D. Grumbach, *Histoires de mode*, Paris: Seuil 1993, p. 245.

demand for individual freedom that will find its expression in the affirmation of individual identity in public life.

This very function of social anticipation can be better understood with the study of some examples. These examples could be drawn from various fields of social survey, but the field of sexual identity, roles and function, as it manifests plainly this power of social anticipation, is certainly the one that needs to be concentrated upon and developed.

"During several centuries, writes Daniel Roche, the two sexes were equal in terms of clothing for refinement and adornment. As a matter of extravagance, from the Renaissance to the Enlightenment, men shone as well as women."[17] But, with the French Revolution, a clothing inequality formalized between the different social orders in the *Ancien Régime* was spontaneously substituted by a far less formalized inequality between the sexes. The sexual clothing division (closed system for men, opened system for women), which has prevailed in the Western world since the Middle Ages, has become even more comprehensive. Indeed, with the 8 Brumaire an II (Oct. 29, 1793) decree that stipulates: "No one of one sex or the other can constrain a citizen to get dressed in a peculiar way upon pain of being regarded and treated as suspect and prosecuted as disturbing public rest: everyone is free to

---

17. D. Roche, *La Culture des apparences. Une histoire du vêtement XVIIe-XVIIIe siècle*, Paris: Points-Seuil, p. 43.

wear the clothes and arrays of one's sex as one wants," the French Revolution abolishes the "lois solitaires," it reinforces sexual dimorphism, as a 16 Brumaire police "ordonnance" forbids Parisian women to wear trousers without special authorization and, consequently, inaugurates a long period in which fashion is only for women and not anymore for men. In the nineteenth century, as we know, the masculine dress is austere, rigid, and dark, a "symbol of an enduring mourning," as Baudelaire depicts it, opposed in every respect to the still colorful and frivolous feminine dress. As the two pipes of the bourgeois trousers replace the aristocratic breeches and stockings, or, more generally, the uniformed or discretely striped suit worn by the "monsieur comme il faut" succeeds the fate of the gentleman's suit, women still shine with any adornment possible, with that new function to signify proxy the social status, the financial power of the father, husband, or lover, who needs to make money without exhibiting it directly, or as Veblen used to put it, to signify "that their master has made it clear that he can pay."[18]

This sexual dimorphism that induces patterns of behavior and representations has contributed to defining, more strongly than ever before in the Western world, the masculine identity and the feminine identity, as Virginia Woolf has stressed in *Orlando*, saying that in clothing lies the essential distinction between the sexes and "often it is only the clothes that keep the male or female likeness, while underneath the sex is the very

---

18. Th. Veblen, *op. cit.*

opposite of what it is above."[19] Nothing can show this better than dandyism protesting against sexual dimorphism.

It is, indeed, as questioning the clothing system that the dandy has to be regarded, the dandy to whom "paraître c'est être (to appear is to be)."[20] And to whom the spirit used to say Marcel Boulanger is his suit. The dandies are protesting against proletarian-bourgeois clothing. But even if, in their protest, there is undoubtedly an aristocratic dimension, they don't stand for a return to the clothing of the "Ancient Régime" but only want to benefit totally from all the new egalitarian values and the virtues of individualism and, consequently, they demand the right to be able, as the women, to compete with faster and elegance. Far more than against egalitarianism, they are protesting against sexual dimorphism. Actually, their protest doesn't ask for, at least with the very first dandies, an imitation of luxurious feminine clothing, let alone a reconsideration of the sexual dimorphism system of clothes - the only feminine array they do adopt being the corset - but simply an alignment on the feminine ways regarding the care for clothing. In fact, they identify themselves with women in their relation to clothes and not in clothes themselves. We know, for instance, that Brummell, the archetype of the dandy, while he pledges for "a masculine simplicity" and rejects "a too feminine

---

19. V. Woolf, *Orlando* (1928), London: The Hogarth Press, 1960, p. 118.

20. J. Barbey d'Aurevilly, *Du dandy et de George Brummell, Oeuvres complètes II*, Paris: Gallimard-Pléiade, p. 703.

attire,"[21] spends, like the most elegant and coquettish women, hours grooming himself to be dressed with the care that could show the rigor, sobriety, and neatness of his suit and attract attention.

Since his way of dressing is a model for society as a whole, the dandy, Brummell and his followers, anticipate the transcendental mediation that, later on, the fashion model will carry on[22] and, consequently, his social efficiency is important. He does contribute to building up an ensemble of collective representations.

If dandyism, quickly neutralized by fashion, had, as a consequence, to decisively consecrate "distinction"[23] that is, as it has often been noticed, the main bourgeois concern[24]. And to announce a time when "fashion is firstly the uniform of elegance."[25] It also helps to define the codes of masculine seduction. Clothes may not determine the internalization of the feminine imprint that is its very essence,[26] but they do accompany it since there is no doubt that they play a large part in the dandy's effemination. Even more. The dandy obviously helps to impose representations of homosexuality that, in the second half of the 19th century, become predominant. Michel Foucault

---

21. F. Coblence, *Le Dandysme, obligation d'incertitude*, Paris: PUF, 1988, p. 116-117.

22. See R. König, *Kleider und Leute, Zur Soziologie der Mode*, 1968.

23. F. Coblence, *op. cit.*, p. 125-126.

24. See Th. Veblen, *op. cit.*, p. 122-123.

25. Yves Saint Laurent, quoted by F. Coblence, *op. cit.* p. 125.

26. See. F. Monneyron, *Séduire. L'Imaginaire de la séduction de Don Giovanni à Mick Jagger*, Paris: PUF, 1997.

underlines that "the psychological, psychiatric, medical category of homosexuality was constituted when it was no more characterized by a particular type of sexual relations but a certain kind of sexual sensitiveness, a certain way of inverting in oneself the masculine and the feminine."[27] Indeed, the *feminine* relation that the dandy, whose sexuality is questioned, entertains with clothes does appear as a model, maybe not unique - art and literature provide other models - but predominant of this inversion.

At the end of the century, the dandy's even stronger alignment with the feminine in his way of dressing coincides with a less censured expression of homosexuality and sometimes supports it, indeed confirming this trend.

The eccentricity that this new type of dandy, the "fin-de-siècle" esthete, manifests in dressing with colors and fabrics (silk, satin, and others) reserved so far to the feminine attire, is, in fact, a way of both hiding and exhibiting the homosexuality that begins then to come out of the closet, and even appearing as a sign of sexual identification. No doubt that literature provides an illustration and even a model of it - let's have in mind, as an example, Dorian Gray's disguises in the chapter XI of Wilde's novel that help to identify some of his outbreaks to come as homosexual.[28] But Wilde's own life could also be regarded as very symbolic. We all

---

27. M. Foucault, *Histoire de la sexualité*, Paris: Gallimard, 1980, p. 59.

28. Should be added his collection of perfumes that in the nineteenth century collective representations and till recently were rerserved to women.

know that his socialite career was interrupted by the scandal linked to his trial for homosexuality. But we often forget that he began this career in protesting, after Walter Pater, against the dullness of 19th century masculine dress.[29] In strolling in London dressed in breeches and stockings, a sunflower in the buttonhole, can't we consider that by reliving the eighteenth-century men's dress and questioning sexual dimorphism, Wilde programs the homosexuality that will cause his fall? By introducing the feminine into the masculine through clothes, he embodies in collective representations this "kind of inner androgyny, of hermaphroditism of the soul" that, according to Foucault,[30] at the end of the 19th century, defined homosexuality, and consequently, because we only exist in the eyes of others, he ends up representing himself as such and being what he looks like. Chronology could help, for sure, to confirm this interpretation of Wilde's homosexuality, since it is usually agreed upon that he becomes a practicing homosexual only at the very end of the 1880s.[31]

---

29. See, on the importance of the masculine dress reformation, the letter written later on by Wilde to the *Daily Telegraph*'s editor: "the uniform black that is worn now, though valuable at a dinner-party, where it serves to isolate and separate women's dresses, to frame them as it were, still is dull and tedious and depressing in itself, and makes the aspect of club-life and men's dinners monotonous and uninteresting."

30. M. Foucault, *op.cit.*, p. 59.

31. See, for instance, the chapter focusing on Oscar Wilde and Lord Alfred Douglas in H. Pearson, *The Life of Oscar Wilde*, London: Methuen and Co, 1954.

If, when protesting against the sexual dimorphism, dandyism contributes to impose the collective representations of distinction, seduction, and homosexuality, a century later the Sixties fashion creation itself emulates representations that anticipate changes in the sexual roles and functions. The extensive use of trousers by women that put an end to the sexual dimorphism and the inception of the mini-skirt that appears as the ultimate stage of the opened system present, indeed, new images of the female.

Trousers, that became a main part of women's wardrobe in the Sixties and Seventies, when, if we consider France, the number of trousers sold to women takes over the number of skirts as soon as 1965 and comes close to the number of dresses in 1971 (fourteen million against fifteen million), promoted the image of a woman who, in borrowing from men their outfit, also got into their professional and social roles. The debates around some previous attempts to introduce trousers as a feminine outfit are good testimonies of this causal relationship.

When Mrs. Bloomer, an American woman, tried to make the bloomer style popular in the United Kingdom in 1851, featuring a shorter skirt and knee-length trousers adorned with laces, she sparked a general outcry. Men considered them an outrage to their prerogatives. *Punch*, a well-known satirical English review and mouthpiece of the middle class, published several pages of humor as an illustration of the dangers of this revolution and of Victorian males' subjection to their wives in breeches.[32] Queen Victoria herself says that "Mrs. Bloomer's trousers were detrimental to the sanctity of British homes and prone to foster both women's emancipation and men's degradation."[33] When, at the turn of the century, trousers for women are to be seen again, with the bicycle, or when the women's dress is getting more masculine with the skirt suit, other voices, no less strong, will rise to suggest, as Edith Sitwell attacking "all these women, dressed in a weird and amorphous masculine attire,"[34] the social and noxious consequences of such a clothing evolution.

On the other hand, feminists never forgot to insist on the importance of clothes. As sexual dimorphism was questioned at the beginning of the twentieth century, when Paul Poiret suppressed the corset, tried to impose Eastern-like trousers under the skirt, and prophesied that "trousers will undoubtedly become a dominant fashion for women,"[35] some of them even fight for a complete takeover of the masculine apparel main characteristics and favor a total indifferentiation. Likewise, one can regard the male Western trousers to be seen on women only in the 1960s as "an attempt to compete with the strong sex on his own turf."[36]

---

32. J. Laver, *Fashion and Costume. A Concise History*, London: Thames & Hudson, 1990, p. 179.

33. M. Toussaint-Samat, *Histoire technique et morale du vêtement*, Paris: Bordas, 1990, p. 379.

34. J. Laver, *op. cit.*

35. See P. Yonnet, *op. cit.*

36. J. Laver, *op. cit.*, p. 269.

For the wearing of pants by women to become the stake - and the engine - of such a rethinking of gender roles, there must at least be a confused sense that, far from being neutral, it changes the way we behave and leads to new ways of being. Indeed, the pants of a woman who is physically constrained by cumbersome garments such as the crinoline, or morally constrained by modesty into a limited number of movements, is contrasted with a woman who can move more easily and is thus free to participate in the same activities as men and, moreover, to behave like them in all areas of social life.

It is assuredly, quite consciously, that the passing from the opened system to the closed system is a hallmark of the conquest by women of men's old prerogatives. However, the shortening of the skirts followed, around 1920, the first attempts to introduce trousers for women, and in the 1960s, the mini-skirt that coincides with their decisive implanting, posing women in their sexual function as the principle of masculine desire, are far less consciously the mark of extreme femininity. The reflection of Mallarmé, who was once asked what he thought of the trousers worn by women riding a bicycle, was already a good introduction to it: "I am, before your question, as before these steel riders, only a passerby who pulls himself back. But if their motive is to show off their legs, I do prefer, from a lifted-up skirt, feminine vertigo, and not from boyish trousers, to be dazzled, upset, and glared."[37] But it is, obviously, the scandal sparked by the adoption of the mini-skirt, invented by Courrèges and popularized by Mary Quant that is the best testimony.[38] To a first degree, maybe superficial, but very symbolic, the mini-skirt manifests something sexual. Indeed, compared to the time when sexuality was buried under the dresses, it represents a breakthrough in which eroticism is linked to a maximum of nakedness and anticipates a society in which sexuality will be exhibited. To a second degree, more profoundly, it encourages Desire to push fashion functions to their ultimate ends. A short detour through psychoanalysis can provide a better understanding.

In this dialectics, "clothes reveal that they are a fake compromise, raising what is refused, in a play in which the other's desire leads the game and only the female modesty is involved. Female modesty is, indeed, the correlate of her duty to stimulate, in the other, the quest for this ultimate intimacy that, since impossible to reveal, supports and draws out his desire."[39] The function of fashion, as a cultural phenomenon, is then to allow the metaphorical introduction of femininity, with no access to language, in the field of representation. Throughout clothes, fashion confers to women the task of stimulating, while hiding it, a part of

---

37. *Ibid.*

38. Discussion remains on this issue. André Courrèges declared: "I did invent the mini-skirt. Mary Quant has only sold the idea», but Mary Quant said she had «another memory of it."

39. H. Rey-Flaud, *Comment Freud inventa le fétichisme... et réinventa la psychanalyse*, Paris: Payot, 1994, p. 140.

the body (arms, shoulders, or breast) to which is devolved the function of representing the unrepresentative point of femininity.[40]

From this function of fashion, we can understand that the miniskirt could appear as an emblem. By unveiling the thighs as largely as possible, it canalizes the eyes, even more than any other piece of clothing that already hides to show, towards the woman's sex that it keeps on to be hidden as well. And since it evokes consequently the absence of what is impossible to represent, it sparks the masculine desire that, though knowing very well that there is nothing to see, can't prevent itself from waiting.[41] In doing so, it also manifests woman as the very principle of the man's desire and sets her in the feminine function of sexual object.

As trousers for women and the mini-skirt have decisively become part of the clothing landscape (the long slit skirt that appeared in the Seventies and was reintroduced from time to time ever since is nothing more than a variation of the latter), they do invite us to consider that the representations they bring forth, and, even the way of behaving they inaugurate, are now part of a contemporary imaginary in which woman is divided between a social function of competitor to man and a sexual function of object of his desire. On the other hand, we have to consider that we can see today, if not the demise of the representations related to

---

40. *Ibid.,* p. 147.

41. *Ibid.*

homosexuality set in the 19th century through the dandy figure, the birth of other representations, closer to the real world of homosexuality, that find again, and this time directly, their very model in a particular way of dressing. Indeed, the birth of a homosexual fashion that picks outfits regarded as virile, in their forms as in their fabrics, plays a large part in the reconsideration of homosexuality as exclusion rather than inclusion of the feminine, and is the ultimate proof of the model and anticipation function of clothes.

CHAPTER 2

THE IMPORTANCE OF DESIGNERS AND SOCIAL MAGAZINES

If clothes have such a power of social anticipation, the social role of the designer is therefore very important.

In traditional societies, tailors often have (or had) a very important social function and a quite particular symbolic value. But that is no more true for his successor: the designer. He is, in our contemporary Western societies, twice underrated. On the one hand, he is the victim of an aesthetic tradition that makes a clear distinction between fine arts and decorative arts, the major arts and the minors, and, consequently, he is never really seen as an artist. The designers themselves very often don't claim to be artists. Coco Chanel used to say, for instance: "Fashion is not an art, but a craft. If art can use fashion, that is already something fine for the glory of fashion"; "it is perfect that a dress could try to equal a beautiful statue, but it can't be a justification for the designers to claim they are artists"; "a dress is not a tragedy, nor a painting, it is a charming and temporary creation, not an everlasting masterpiece. Fashion has to die and die quickly so that trade could go on."[42] On the other hand, the designer is bound to a Christian morality that distinguishes the body from the soul and regards the care granted to the body as detrimental to the salvation of the soul. Consequently, everything that has to do with adornment is considered an activity, if not entirely shallow, at least secondary, and the designer is not seen as a true businessman and manufacturer.

However, this lack of consideration is a strange paradox. Indeed, the designer is just at the crossroads between the world of art and the world of trade, and in Western societies, since the end of the 19th century with Charles-Frederick Worth, he occupies in fact a very important position. According to some authors, this position could be compared to the position of the poet in Antiquity. He is the one who creates pure beauty, who is listening to the world, who guesses what the women want to wear far before they are themselves conscious of it, before they formulate it to themselves.[43] His fame, since the Second World War, is still more important. It is grounded on the location of his house, on the quality of the public at his shows. But, today when a designer is successful, no doubt that his fame as a creator is far more important than the fame of the top creators in art, literature, or music. And his financial results as a businessman are by no means lower than those of industries regarded as more fundamental. Which writer, which artist, which movie-makers sees

---

42. P. Morand, *L'Allure Chanel*, Paris: Hermann, 1976, p. 140.

43. M. Rouff, *La Philosophie de l'élégance*, Paris: Editions littéraires, 1942, p. 240-241.

one's own name so widely exposed to the eyes of the crowd, on the shops of our cities or on any piece of clothes? And, on the contrary, which businessman may expect to gain the fame of an activity associated nevertheless to art?

But, beyond this in-between position that puts him forth in many different ways (designers such as Karl Lagerfeld or Jean-Paul Gaultier have obviously become stars), the social importance of the designer comes from one's ability to create patterns – I should say models in every sense of the word. Yves Saint Laurent has put it that way : "Fashion is a change in women's attitudes ; I am trying with my own humble means to transform women's attitudes." And if, as I have suggested previously, creation in the field of clothes anticipates and most generally, determines social changes in modifying the images of the body, and, therefore, the behaviors, then the designer is worth the attention of the sociologist.

Some will say that haute couture, the most famous part of fashion in which the designer has moved in priority so far has not enough customers (some one hundred and fifty persons in the whole world for all the fashion houses) and too small an audience to provide patterns. But this argument is not peremptory.

Firstly, we may answer that the coming up of whatever object as a model has nothing to do with the importance of the audience, but if we refer to Gabriel de Tarde, with the superiority given to the one who owns this object, and that explains why Haute Couture, aiming at people who are privileged by birth, money, beauty, and envied for that: actors, princes, singers, etc., is by essence something to be imitated. Coco Chanel used to insist on the fact that fashion has to be born in luxury, for "luxury is the genius of the artist able to conceive and to give form," and that "this form, then, is expressed, translated, and disseminated by millions of women who abide by it."[44] But there are simply some new directions in forty years. As Jean-Paul Gaultier puts it: "Every period had its stars who influenced their fans in their way of dressing," but today "the rock stars have more influence than anybody else."[45] John Stephen, who owned several shops in Sixties London, noticed that when the Beatles or the Rolling Stones chose particular clothes, their fans wanted to be dressed the same way as soon as possible.[46] More recently, Marc Jacobs, the American designer for Louis Vuitton, insisted on the fact that "people like the clothes that make them look like a star."[47] Anyway, the stars are generally very powerful means of dissemination as far as clothes are concerned.

There is no doubt that the audience of haute couture was quite small from the beginning, but thanks to fashion photography, television and cinema, it can very well impose its patterns on a larger number of people. In addition to the direct representations of catwalk

---

44. See D. Grumbach, *op.cit.*, p. 132.

45. See V. Steele, *Se Vêtir au XXe siècle. De 1945 à nos jours*, Paris: Adam Biro, p. 169.

46. *Ibid.*, p. 71.

47. *Ibid.*, 169.

shows - in magazines, on television, and today also on the Internet - indirect representations can take place through fashion photography, television and films. Film costumes, theater or ballet costumes, for example, are often a good opportunity for designers to express their talent and promote their brand; they can also use the clothes of a singer or a TV presenter to promote their brand. Sometimes a movie is even about their own creation, as with Paco Rabanne's metallurgy dresses in the famous sixties movie Who are you, Polly Magoo?

At last, I shall stress the fact that today, this debate no longer makes sense. Since the Sixties at least, the craftsmanship and uniqueness of Haute Couture have evolved into the industrial reproduction in series of ready-to-wear (today all Haute Couture designers have their ready-to-wear).[48] In the mid sixties, many had even forecast the death of the Haute Couture. Emmanuelle Kahn, in 1964, declared: "The Haute Couture is dead. I want to reach the women I cross in the street" and Pierre Cardin has as an objective in 1967 "to reach the entire world and not only fifty women." As to Yves Saint Laurent, one of the first great designers to get interested in ready-to-wear, in the same years, he was sure that the Haute Couture would not live more than four or five years, and Emmanuel Ungaro said that the Haute Couture needed to be killed. As a dying person, the Haute Couture is rather resilient

---

48. The best recent example is Christian Lacroix, who enjoyed in 1987 a great success with his Haute Couture collections, but had at that time nothing else to sell and quickly signs agreements to start a luxury ready-to-wear.

and is not doing that bad. And with the revelation of Christian Lacroix's collections in 1987, one even spoke of its renaissance. B. Morris wrote, then, in *The New York Times* that Christian Lacroix has relived the Haute Couture, while Lolly Brubach affirmed in *The New Yorker* in 1988 that the Haute Couture has regained its prestige and that its activity is quite strong. And Yves Saint Laurent recognized later on that, after all, it plays an important social role in embodying luxury and imagination. But it is even more important to notice that, today, the distinction between Haute Couture and ready-to-wear is no longer valid and that they have more or less merged into each other in what had been called the Creation, which, as Pierre Cardin noted, partakes of both but not one or the other ; it just gives to the former the means of its revival and to the latter the totality of its inspiration; it offers elegance while reaching a larger amount of customers.[49]

Another objection seems even stronger. Many authors would admit that fashion creates models that are to be imitated, but they would object that, today, these models don't come anymore from the studios of the great designers, but right from the street. Anyway, this objection is not so easy to accept. That doesn't

---

49. Yet, distinct runway shows have remained eversince: January and July for the Haute Couture, March and October for the ready-to-wear, even if after André Courrèges who had merged his Haute Couture and ready-to-wear collections in Spring 1966, Yves Saint Laurent, Pierre Cardin and Nina Ricci try in April 1972 to reunite their shows or if, twenty years later, Thierry Mugler and Emmanuel Ungaro seek to insert the show of their ready-to-wear collections into the Haute Couture agenda (D. Grumbach, *op. cit.*, p 228 and p. 246-247).

mean that the street can't create new style in fashion. That just means that what was born in the street - product of individual revolt or, most of the time, creation that defines the identity of different groups of young people claiming that they belong to some different forms of counter-culture or sub-culture - can't stand for itself and doesn't constitute in its street form a model to be imitated. It is quite true, indeed, as says Ted Polhemus, in *Street Style. From Sidewalk to Catwalk,* that "without the Hipsters, Teddy Boys, Beats, Rockers, Rude Boys, Mods, Surfers, Hippies, Punks, B. Boys, Fly girls, Raggamuffins – and all the other street style originals – most of us would be left without anything to wear."[50] But to become a model that can be imitated by the masses, all these street style originals need the mediation of the designer. They need the mediation of the designer to express, as Coco Chanel used to say "the fashion that walks in the street without knowing it just exists". This mediation is, actually, a transposition, an adaptation and a purification, and it just takes into account habits and restraints as well as a desire for something new.

In the last decades, the designers themselves openly praised the street. For instance, Mary Quant, in competition with André Courrèges as the inventor of the miniskirt, said: "Neither André Courrèges nor I got

---

50. T. Polhemus, *Street Style. From Sidewalk to Catwalk,* London and New York: Thames and Hudson, 1994, p. 6.

the idea of the miniskirt. The street invented it."[51] And Yves Saint Laurent, in May 1968, declared: "Down the Ritz, live the street."[52] But the situation is, indeed, far more complex. Both Mary Quant and Yves Saint Laurent got the intuition it was. Mary Quant added that "designers only anticipate what the public wants. Courrèges may have invented the miniskirt but if he did, nobody wore it." And Yves Saint Laurent's conclusion was : "Between the street and I, it's a love story". In saying so, he just admitted a kind of reciprocity and, one year later, he will insist on the interaction between the street and the designer: "When I initiated trousers for women, he said, I did nothing new. The young women did not wait for me to wear trousers." I shall sum up in saying that from the Sixties till now, it is quite true that some styles were created by younger generations in the street, but that it was after those styles had been adopted by great designers who modified and adapted them somehow they could be sold to the masses. There are many examples of it. It is quite obvious that it is once they have been reworked by a designer that some of the traditional clothes still worn in everyday life in Africa or Asia could be worn in the Western world. It is quite true too that the success of clothes in the cities of Europe or America is bound to the ability of the designer to transform it into fashion. For instance, there

---

51. See R. Lynam, *Couture, An Illustrated History of the Great Paris Designers and their Creatures,* Garden City NY : Doubleday and Co, 1972.

52. Quoted in Vincent-Ricard, *Raison et passion 1940-1960*, Paris: Ed. Textile-Art, Langage, 1983, p. 28.

is little doubt that the hippy style would not have been adopted by many people and gained a large market if top designers had not adopted it first and slightly modified it. In its triumph in France at the beginning of the Seventies someone as Jean Bouquin, who used to dress Brigitte Bardot, has played an important part. One decade later, the punk style – to which most of the consumers were still more hostile than to the hippy style – had to be tamed by Vivienne Westwood to become, if not a fashion, at least a state of mind which will govern fashion in the Eighties and the Nineties. And, undoubtedly, we must interpret that the Grunge, born in the streets of Seattle, has failed to create any true fashion as the the designers were unable to carry on any transformation. The attempt of a psychedelic version of the Grunge by Dolce and Gabbana and Gianni Versace was obviously too shy.

The evolution of fashion, as well as the dialectics between the street and the studio, make it clear that the designer creates models and plays a crucial part in societal dynamics. However, in the field of fashion, creation is, to a large extent, a collective endeavor, making the social importance of the designer even stronger. When speaking of "collective creation" it is not just about several individuals working together to build a collection. It also goes beyond the fact that today, in publications like *Vogue* or other fashion magazines, clothes from different designers can be found in the same photo-shoot. It refers to something less obvious: in the realm of fashion, different models are often encapsulated in a larger model or a smaller number of models that distinctly represent a historical period at first glance. Designers, guided by a mysterious *Zeitgeist*, tend to follow a common trend. "Had not Christian Dior existed, other designers such as Jacques Fath, Pierre Balmain, Jean Dessès would have gone in the same direction. They will have invented the New Look anyway" says a commentator. And Sonia Rykiel points out that, "at the same time, without speaking to each other the designers have collections with similar themes." Why ? Because, she answers, "they react to the same things at the same moment, a movie, a book, a happiness or a - drama in the world."[53]

All this, of course, justifies a sociological approach. Moreover, the imagery of clothes and fashion is a privileged access to underground movements and trends of a period, trends that give this period its atmosphere and style. Fashion may very well be shallow, but this shallowness has many virtues, for this shallowness figures - better: prefigures - the coming state of a society. Chanel would not have denied it, who regarded, at least a posteriori, her first strange hats, "so dry and severe (...) as a prefiguration of the iron age to come but not yet announced."[54]

Images, in the Western philosophical tradition, are definitely not seen as positive. This mistrust originates in the Middle Ages. The medieval Aristotelianism

---

53. Quoted by P. Mauriès, *Sonia Rykiel*, Paris: Assouline, 1997.

54. Quoted in P. Morand, *op. cit.*, p. 37.

coming from the Arab philosopher Averroes was an apology of the direct way of thinking against the indirect way of thinking[55], namely the way of thinking through myths and images. And, accordingly, the *Mundus imaginalis* disappeared, and rationalism became the very basis of our philosophical tradition. This tradition has tried to point out how images can be false and what kind of impact images can have on our senses and our passions. During the Renaissance and the Classical Age, philosophers, following Plato who used to distinguish between images that are a criterion of value and truth and images that are simulation, stressed on the capacity of images to create illusions that make us believe in the reality of appearances.[56] Later on, Kant linked the loss of consciousness or even the loss of reason to the power of images which make us slide from daydream to hallucination.

This philosophical position concerning images, which, according to the German sociologist Max Weber, the Reformation has encouraged and intensified, is today in question. Parallel to the technical development that promotes images through photography, cinema, and television, some contemporary thinkers have tried to rehabilitate images as a medium between sensitivity and intellect. To quote some: Gaston Bachelard, Mircea Eliade, Gilbert Durand. And if this rehabilitation is far from being over, at least some methods to analyze images have

---

55. G. Durand, *L'Imagination symbolique*, Paris: PUF, 1989, p. 29-30.

56. J.-J. Wunenberger, *Philosophie des images*, Paris: PUF, 1997, p. 254.

been provided. But a new debate has been introduced. In a Western civilization that has become a civilization of images, their very proliferation raises some new questions. And without even considering, as Jean Baudrillard suggests, that this leads to a confusion between reality and image,[57] many are those who regard this proliferation as quite dangerous.

Anyway, in the rehabilitation of images as well as in this debate, fashion is a very good field of survey.

If fashion illustrates the contemporary importance of images, fashion also asserts quite clearly the social power of images. As we have seen, as far as clothes are concerned, the imaginary doesn't only determine the social but is a prefiguration of it. More. Fashion appears as a modern ersatz of this *mundus imaginalis* denied by modernity and, indeed, retrieves some of its very functions. Most particularly, fashion conciliates collective dimension and symbolic depth.

Actually, fashion images reach all of us and are seen in everyday life, but they also carry a deep meaning that was previously considered to be that of literary and artistic creation, reserved for an elite with limited social function. In other words, fashion, thanks to its images, has a broad and popular audience while it has evolved into a true art form with all the functions of an art form. The fashion figures and images may hold the same importance today as the popular and religious figures in

---

57. Cf. J. Baudrillard, *De la séduction*, Paris: Galilée, 1979 or *La Guerre du Golfe n'a pas eu lieu*, Paris : Galilée, 1991.

ancient times, as fashion showcases flesh, modesty, chastity, temptation, pleasure, and eroticism.

Fashion images are supported by different media. There are the fashion shows in themselves where many aesthetic elements are bound together: the designer's personal vision of beauty, the new inventions of the textile industry, the handcraft of the Haute Couture, the technology of ready-to-wear, the choice of the girls, and the current taste for such type of beauty… But it is very difficult for the sociologist to take into account the only visual impressions told by the happy few who attend the shows. In compensation, the representation of the shows on TV could be considered. Some networks, especially in the United States, present the shows in their totality. But that is far too recent to be efficient on a long-term approach. Not to mention TV, the shows were not recorded on video before the early Eighties. Before, only photographs are available. And no need to consider the Internet, which is even newer. Consequently, for a general survey of fashion images, we have to concentrate on a more traditional medium: fashion magazines. More particularly on women's fashion magazines, for men's fashion shows as men's fashion magazines are, here again, far too recent.

Fashion magazines have, indeed, very important social functions. First, they make a selection among the different clothes seen on the catwalk and, consequently, because they are just in-between the designer and the customer, they decide what will be the clothes of the year. Even if a mysterious *Zeitgeist* makes most of the designers go in the same trend, the mission of the fashion journalists and the photographers, even if they are not aware of it, is to take everything in a particular designer that goes in that trend and to leave apart everything that doesn't go in the trend. Second, as far as fashion photography is concerned, in associating a girl, a landscape and a situation to a particular piece of clothes in a determined photographic style, the fashion magazines create an atmosphere, which identifies a period.

This is the social function of all the fashion magazines, but no doubt that some magazines such as *Vogue, Harper's Bazaar, Women's Wear Daily,* or *Elle* were and are indeed more important than others. Consequently, an in-depth study of fashion images could not help but deal with these magazines. *Vogue*, in particular, may be regarded as a real gold mine and an essential tool for the sociologist of fashion. In the Fifties and Sixties, "the lines were set by magazine editors for magazine readers. *Vogue* used to announce the color of a season, and, up and down the land, shops presented clothes in banana beige or coral red or whatever" wrote Peter York in *Modern Times.*[58] And, if today *Vogue* shares this function with other magazines, it surely still has it. Insomuch as it has been modernized and as its pages often come to resemble those of *The Face* and *I-D,*[59] it may even reach a larger audience.

---

58. P. York, *Modern Times,* London: 1994, p. 10.

59. T. Polhemus, *op. cit.,* p. 12.

II. FASHION IMAGES AND SOCIAL FIGURES

CHAPTER 3

SPACE AND TIME

In the fashion images from which Western designers can find inspiration, ethnic clothes undoubtedly play quite an important part.

As far as clothing is concerned, it is true that the Western world has always borrowed from somewhere else, but up to the nineteen sixties, almost exclusively fabrics were borrowed from Africa, Asia, or America: silk, cotton, later chinchilla or sable furs, or the ethnic aspect was reduced to some accessories. In short, it did not touch the very essence of the European costume, what identifies it at first sight: its cut, its colour, and its sexual dimorphism. And we know that Paul Poiret's attempt, at the beginning of the twentieth century, to impose on women Eastern-like trousers, a sort of harem pants, was a failure or that, later on, Elsa Schiaparelli's attempt to promote the Indian sari or even a dhoti-inspired shirt was quite restricted. But, since the nineteen sixties, entire parts of the wardrobe of other civilizations have entered into the Western wardrobe. Some may interpret this phenomenon as the consequences of the ready-to-wear success and may even see in it a new frivolity of fashion that, once all the combinations in the Western system of dressing have been experienced, seeks elsewhere something new. But this frivolity is far deeper and more instructive than we may think.

All the clothes that we call "ethnic" in today's language of fashion figure our relation to the Other and, to an extent, inform us, possibly better than any other artistic creation, on the way we see other cultures. On the one hand, they express, indeed, a genuine opening to the whole world, but on the other hand, this opening only exists from a particular perspective and finality. The transformation of this kind of clothes so that they could fit Western habits betrays, more than anything else, the way we see the Other.

Some other elements accompany this opening to the whole world, expressed by ethnic clothes. Both the Japanese designers who appeared on the Parisian fashion scene in the sixties, such as Hanae Mori, or in the seventies, such as Kenzo or Issey Miyake,[60] and the African models who were to be seen on the catwalks at the end of the seventies.[61] But the Japanese designers have mainly worked for the European market and are close to its norms, while the African models wear European clothes. Accordingly, they don't significantly

---

60. Kenzo is keen of being related to exoticism, since he paints his first shop in the Galerie Vivienne with jungle motifs close to Douanier Rousseau's and names his ready-to-wear *Jungle Jap.*

61. They can be found on Yves Saint Laurent's catwalks in 1977, even if Courrèges, Givenchy and Ungaro have claimed to be the very first ones to have introduced them in the world of Western fashion.

modify the European fashion images. But, by their very presence, they are illustrative of the desire to break Western norms and, at least, they spray on the catwalks a fragrance of Africa or Asia.

This desire to break the Western norms is nevertheless better expressed by the clothes themselves. Fashion may very well be, in the Sixties and the Seventies, where new exoticism is now to be found. In a world where exoticism is no longer in literature or even in the movies, clothes are just a new form of it: the otherness is worn on the bodies themselves and in everyday life. The designers, through a particular type of clothing, express the modern desire for adventure: the well-known "saharienne" (safari jacket) by Yves Saint Laurent, worn in 1968 by the famous top model Veruschka, a rifle on her shoulder in a Franco Rubartelli photograph, is, of course, a perfect example of it. On another side, the designers are looking everywhere in the world for something new. Some collections have, indeed, their origins in the art of Black Africa, such as the Yves Saint Laurent "Bambara collection" in 1967, or some dresses by Christian Lacroix in 1988, or even, more recently, some dresses inspired by John Galliano for Christian Dior by the Massais in Kenya. But, generally, the main inspiration of the designers is definitely what was called, in the nineteenth century, the Eastern world: from North Africa and Russia to Japan and China, passing through India and Afghanistan. This restriction is quite significant. As the Eastern world is, in Western imagination, the reverse of the Western world rather than an absolute Otherness, the same as well as the other, it is a land of repulsion as well as a land of fascination.[62]; and, accordingly, the Eastern world is also an everlasting temptation. The values that are regarded as Eastern values are, actually, the values that have been repressed or rejected by the Western world, and, therefore, they have a very important power of revolt and a lot of potential. And it is the case of the clothes that the designers borrow from traditional Eastern clothes: they appear at first sight as the symbolic expression of all these values.

In the late sixties, the creation of the designers was as much a creation coming from the street; the hippie fashion is a perfect example. Hippie clothes told us about imaginary travels. They borrowed quite a lot from Morocco on the one hand, and from Afghanistan and India on the other hand. At that time, the meaning of Moroccan caftans and harem pants, Indian shirts and dresses, and Afghan coats and jackets was clearly a desire for communion and spirituality that a generation at odds with the Western values of individualism and materialism tried to find in Eastern mysticism and, that is not contradictory, in drugs, for drugs and clothes were coming then from the same Eastern places. The external appearances are just coherent with a counter-culture that is interested in Sufism, Hinduism, and Buddhism and borrows from the Eastern cultures the smoking of kif or hashish, just as if before getting into the beliefs and ways of life of one civilization, one ought

---

62. See E. W. Said, *Orientalism,* London: Penguin Classics, 1972.

to get firstly into its clothes. No doubt that many of us would regard this fashion as a simple imitation of the Easterners' appearance without getting fundamentally into their beliefs and ways of life. But we have to admit that this fashion coming from the East is a sign, maybe superficial but explicit, of a quest.

In the same years, some other fashion creations, even if they don't fit within this attraction/repulsion scheme of the East, are other good examples. The Pierre Cardin so-called "veste à col Mao," Mao collar jacket, was not a lasting success. Nevertheless, it betrays a genuine fascination for Mao's China, a fascination that was not, indeed, only Pierre Cardin's. Moreover, while the Indian or Moroccan ethnic clothes of the hippy fashion appear as symbols of philosophical and societal options, the Mao collar jacket has definitely a more political dimension. It exhibits Chinese communism as the only true alternative to Western capitalism against which a younger generation is at odds. It was even clearer that ideological positions were expressed through clothes when, at the beginning of the Seventies, some French fashion journalists praised and wore Chinese working clothes, those of the poor coolie, as a symbol of their fight against capitalism.

The choice, in modern fashion, of elements belonging to the Eastern way of dressing means more, as we see, than a simple revolt against the Western way of dressing. It just sums up and illustrates the revolt against a whole way of thinking, of being together, and even a revolt against a whole organization of production and work. But, as many buyers and wearers of ethnic clothes were (quite a lot for the hippie fashion, only some for Pierre Cardin's outfit), ethnic clothes were transformed, and a complete work of redefinition was carried out.

Let us have, as an example, the clothes that the hippies brought back from Morocco, Afghanistan, and India. There is little doubt that they had a large success in everyday life because they lost, partly or totally, their power of symbolization. I mean that they had been largely accepted only when the symbol had no more sense, when what the symbol symbolized had been forgotten. Then, Morocco or India are not anymore this temptation of the Western world, a fascinating as well as a threatening universe, but just an exotic universe with bright colors and splendid fabrics. And very soon afterwards, to get dressed in an Indian shirt or a Moroccan caftan doesn't mean anymore to be open to the whole world, but only to be a fashion victim. We can understand, therefore, that once they have been deprived of their very first meaning, all these fashion images become part of the fashion memory and are prone to be used again. There were, indeed, some attempts in the winter of '92-'93 to relive the hippy fashion, as well as those, more recently, of Gucci and Anna Sui. Certainly. But generally, the Sixties' exotic choices let the way open to clothes that don't mean anything else but lust, refinement, and luxury, possibly the only vision of Morocco or India the Western world can really tolerate. In several of Yves Saint Laurent's

Haute Couture collections, the magnificence clearly overcomes any other consideration, as in the "Indian collection" in 1982 featuring the Indian top model Kirat or his collections "Hommage" to Delacroix or to Bakst, mostly made out of very beautiful Moroccan fabrics. Likewise, this Eastern inspiration is quite obvious in the Haute Couture collections during the winter of '88-'89 (Dior, Féraud, Scherrer) as well as in the ready-to-wear collections in the spring of 1993, from Chanel to Versace and Dolce and Gabbana.

The transforming process that deprives the exotic clothes of their original meaning is even clearer when we focus on the Mao collar jacket. When we consider it quite precisely, Pierre Cardin's outfit is very far from being a revolt against the capitalist societies of the Western world and an apology of Maoist China, the paradise of the working class. The Mao collar jacket itself is already a transformation. It certainly is a revolt against some Western dressing habits such as the tie, which has been the rule for Western males for more than a century,[63] but it had no other ambition and fundamentally partakes of the Western world values. Indeed, even if we don't want to see some irony in Pierre Cardin's vision of Mao's China, we shall all agree to say that, far from meaning the hard work of the factories or the rice fields, Pierre Cardin's Mao collar jacket just means, on the contrary, leisure, to speak in

---

63. More recently, this revolt has again been carried on, with different meaning, by Gianni Versace. See G. Versace's book, *Men without Ties*, New York, Paris, London: Abbeville Press 1997.

Veblen's terms. Even more, it doesn't mean uniformity of the human condition and equality before work, but it just means distinction, distinction which was in the nineteenth century the only way to singularisation for men, as the dandy exemplified, since all the male clothes were basically all the same. This is quite obvious in the reformulation of the Mao collar jacket by Thierry Mugler in the early Eighties, and particularly in a well-known anecdote. Jack Lang, the socialist minister of culture, came at that time in the French Parliament wearing a Mao collar jacket by Thierry Mugler. It was scandalous to many people, but no one in France interpreted it as the apology of a political system. All the contrary. What was scandalous was this unacceptable distinction for a congressman, at least in that particular place where you should wear the ugly trousers-jacket uniform *with a tie...*

The clothes borrowed by the Western world from the Eastern one are significant of the way the former sees the latter. First, these clothes are very good witnesses of the values that we think of as being the other civilization's values; and, second, once transformed in regard to the norms of the Western world, they are quite significant of the cultural and political logics of our civilizations. There is still a third perspective.

Two very famous Haute Couture collections in the Seventies made it clear that the Eastern world was no longer the mystical and political dreams of the Western world, nor the Eastern world transformed and mastered in a Western way (in a word: westernized), but an Eastern world as an expression of some Western phantasms. Yves Saint Laurent's very famous 1976 Haute Couture collection: "Opéra Ballets russes (Russian Ballets)", as well as the "Opium" collection for the 1978 summer, were devoted to Russia and China. However, they were not devoted to today's Russia and China, but to an older Russia and China, basis to all fantasies.

The very luxurious clothes, most of the time black and red, with smooth and large forms of the Russian Ballet's collection (at that time the most expensive show ever seen in Paris)[64] build up the image of a Russia of fantasy, a paradise of luxury and lust. One hundred and ten models: mink chapkas and golden-leather boots, multicolored "babushka" dresses, long gypsy silk and taffeta skirts, golden-threaded and sable-adorned Cossack coats, velvet boleros, camisoles, and bustiers, etc., that were called by commentators "rich peasant style." In the "Opium" collection, the rich peasant style was opposed to the poor peasant style, namely to the one the Mao collar jacket was supposed to represent. This new collection is, indeed, as luxurious as the "Russian Ballets," and the clothes are supposed to be the magnificent clothes of Imperial China.

But in both collections, Russia and China are, actually, quickly forgotten. On the one hand, because

---

64. The shows were performed so far at Yves Saint Laurent fashion house's, Avenue Marceau, and it was the first time the show took place at the Intercontinental Hotel in Paris and had a very precise staging.

Yves Saint Laurent doesn't mind historical correctness; on the other hand, because they are an invitation to a far more marvellous trip, a trip into the imaginary of a period. The images that we keep in mind are images of decay and chaos where opulence, violence, and destruction are intimately linked together. It is also another image of the woman, quite at odds with the one that prevailed in the previous decade, which is promoted. Now she is an unreachable goddess, a femme fatale, or a kept girl of the harem (some women of the Russian collection, although in leather boots, appeared in a photo shoot for *Vogue* by Guy Bourdin as *Les Femmes d'Alger* by Delacroix. And those of the Chinese collection just appear as some prisoners submitted to their all-time masters and admirers). She can also be the Great Goddess of the mythologies, or a Belle Dame sans merci, or even Mrs. Butterfly; in short: images of this dangerous and dominant femininity that the fashion of the next decade would be made of.

This Eastern world, which carries all the Western fears and obsessions, we shall find it back twenty years later in Jean-Paul Gaultier's stunning and beautiful winter 1994-1995 collection, the so-called "Mongol" collection. As in Yves Saint Laurent's collections, Russia and China, Mongolia, that country in between those two great neighbors that no one ever talks about, is here again a mere pretext. Playing with the historical characteristics attached to the Mongols, those of a population of the steppes, violent and nomadic, bringing destruction and violence, Jean-Paul

Gaultier suggests in this collection a universe of wildness. And, indeed, the clothes he creates don't give the image of a decadent world but - other times, other imaginary - the image of a world after the decadence, where nothing, or almost nothing, is still alive. The tunics and the fur coats, the heavy jewels of old style, the animal skin jackets produce an impression of a world that has come back to a primitive state, full of violence and cruelty, consequently to a kind of bestiality that we can't forget despite the sophisticated aspect of the whole image.

Jean-Paul Gaultier may be inspired by the East, but he takes some distance and deploys a lot of irony. In his winter 1988-1989 ready-to-wear collection, his inspiration comes from China and Vietnam, but he makes fun of his own inspiration by mixing it with other influences such as Klimt paintings or panther motifs, or by interpreting it in his own way: "This Vietnamese figure is not likely to be found in Vietnam. Cut like male clothes, but slit the entire length, the frock forms are quite close to Vietnamese tunics. As the collection takes form, I confuse the issue to do what is most convenient, and these slits were indeed convenient since they accentuate the hips, as do the low-waisted trousers, my very obsession then."[65] His collection called "Rabbins chics" (the chic Rabbins) for the winter of 1993-1994 is still more illustrative, as are his more recent kimonos. With them, he really caricatures the exotic theme. He doesn't transform Eastern clothes to Western norms

---

65. J-P. Gaultier in *Vogue*, France, February 1989, p. 158.

but casts the Western values of elegance and distinction on the traditional clothes of the Brooklyn Hasidic Jews or the Japanese, who ignore these values.

As footnotes to the above, I would like to consider at last another kind of exoticism, which deals with time instead of space.

The time dimension can be seen in many fashion images that are familiar with the exotic theme – Yves Saint Laurent's Imperial China, for instance– but the relation to time appears in itself as one of the main relations in contemporary fashion.

We could, of course, find this relation indirectly in all the constraints that the memory of fashion, as it may be called, impose on every designer. Indeed, a designer can never get rid of what was there before him, and even when he rebels against something, he still summons it somehow.

But the relation to time is still more obvious in the images of ancient clothes, which are a constant inspiration for today's designers. As Ralph Lauren puts it: "Fashion demands always something new, but everything comes from the past."[66] Yet, this journey through the past is not the only relation to time. This relation is definitely richer than we could imagine, for it includes the future, and the everlasting present is a constant inspiration for fashion. But let me explain these two points. Fashion, since the Sixties, on the one

---

66. Quoted by V. Steele, *Fetish; Fashion, Sex and Power*, New York, Paris, London: Abbeville Press, 1997, p. 83.

hand, has always tried to project into the future, from André Courrèges' "space uniforms" to the "techno clothes" in the last years and, on the other hand, has always privileged youth as a major inspiration.

Let us stress this second point. The constitution, in the Sixties, of youth as a social category – the last step in the building up, in the nineteenth century, of youth as a transition age between the child and the adult world – is a way of keeping death away, for there is no doubt that in our contemporary societies, death is more and more scandalous to the people. And today, fashion, which is linked to the constitution of youth as a social category, is even much more illustrative of this desire to keep death away. The Sixties fashion is clearly to be regarded as an attempt to say life in its strength and plenitude, as a desire for everlasting youth. What may be expressed, for instance, by the invention of the miniskirt, this outfit borrowed from the wardrobe of children, is a desire to stop time, the process of becoming, and to stay in the innocence of the origins. Likewise, the dropping of bras, before being interpreted as a liberation from the constraints on the female body, then as an erotic pose, has to be seen as an alignment of the adult woman with the little girl's way of being and, consequently, as a return to childhood.

This desire to stop time can be seen as well in the following decades. But rather than borrowing from the children, it will be carried on through other means. For example, by mixing different historical periods in a single piece of clothing, as the designers of the Eighties and the Nineties will do. Actually, it is even more a desire to annihilate time than to stop it, which may be somehow different. Some Christian Lacroix and Jean-Paul Gaultier's clothes are quite remarkable in that respect. The famous dress by Christian Lacroix in the 1987-1988 Haute Couture collection, called "La Cigale" (the Cicada), is a mix of the seventeenth-century Arles traditional costumes and a Fifties dress. Or this astonishing Jean-Paul Gaultier dress in 1995, which is a mix of several periods: a ballroom dress inspired by the Fifties, early nineteenth-century boots, fox fur from the Forties, and a T-shirt from the Nineties. To an extent, Grunge may also be interpreted as entwining different periods but in a more desperate, negative way, as an annihilation of time, to be sure, but as an annihilation that knows we can't ever get rid of it.

When fashion doesn't annihilate or stop time, it can very well get out of it. Since the beginning of the twentieth century, fashion seems to be perpetually sliding away from the present, either in finding inspiration in the clothes of the past or in trying to imagine what the clothes of the future may look like. This looking backwards or forwards may be regarded as the denial of reality and, consequently, as the will to seek refuge, through clothes, in the values of another historical period. But this may very well be too the interpretation of one period by another.

The first point can be seen in what has been called the "retro" fashion of the Nineties. It could be regarded as an attempt to escape from the present time. Accordingly, it should also be interpreted as the expression of a true difficulty to live and to be. To go back to a past that could be as well the Twenties, the Thirties, the Forties, the Fifties (the "retro" strictly speaking) but also the Renaissance, the eighteenth century, the Directory period in France, the "Belle Époque," and even the more recent Sixties and Seventies —in short, everything a very difficult everyday life could be forgotten with— has to be regarded as a desperate quest for evasion and dreams.

On the contrary, both the futurism of the Sixties and a particular collection significant of the general trend of the Seventies should be regarded as an interpretation of the present by the past. The meaning of André Courrèges' space costumes, Paco Rabanne's space warrior metallic dresses, and the psychedelic-inspired clothes may not imply a complete faith in the world to come but, at least, a real hope in technological progress and a true confidence in the future. The "Années 40 (Forties)" collection inspired by Yves Saint Laurent in 1971 by Paloma Picasso, Pablo Picasso's daughter, was such a great surprise to everyone,[67] highlights a break in the progressive Sixties while inventing the "retro" and is a definition of the coming decade. The Seventies will be both past and future-oriented. They will be a pause in the progressive

---

67. Some journalists left the Rue Spontini, where the Saint Laurent fashion house was then located before the end of the show while in February 1971, *Time Magazine* headlines "Yves of destruction" and the *Houston Post*, in March 1971: "Is this an ugly way to look?"

experience and an attempt to balance those experiences with the values of the past. Even more, the collection just builds a bridge between the years to come and the post-World War II years. The post-war years were years of an aspiration to come back to everyday life and also years of an intense desire, after the tragedy of the war, to live plainly one's own life; and the years to come are quite similarly an aspiration to find a calmer rhythm in one's own life after the effervescent Sixties, but also a desire to drive to the end of the roads that the Sixties had opened up.

More punctually, the Karl Lagerfeld eighteenth-century inspiration in 1977, the Gianni Versace Renaissance inspiration in 1981, or, all along the Eighties, the Thierry Mugler science fiction inspiration do define the trends of a period. Thus, the eighteenth-century reference can be regarded as triply characterizing the last years of the Seventies: in placing them under the sign of the Ancien Régime splendour in adornment and fabrics; under the sign of a clothing faste equal for men and women; and a certain wantonness. Likewise, calling in the Italian Renaissance, there is little doubt that Gianni Versace suggests a world of violence and sensuousness as a world of art, elegance, and refinement that could characterize the Eighties. And the Thierry Mugler "intergalactic" inspiration that retrieves a former space inspiration — this "*Fashion for future*," as it is depicted in the magazine *Interview*— would picture the decade as a technology decade and a decade with faith in progress.

However, this relation to time developed by fashion is not always as direct. Most often, the designers just deprive any value from the reference to a definite historical period - at best, they just try to create a special atmosphere by referring to a particular period. "French culture is my own folklore. The eighteenth-century Europe is, to me, a source of inspiration that others get in Afghanistan," declares Karl Lagerfeld to define his 1977 collection that, far from being representative of the eighteenth century, is certainly refined, but also "of secret and straight femininity, private and not public," and with such futility "that the vulgarity and the materialistic side of our time is to be hidden."[68] Another example is Gianni Versace, who admitted that his 1981 collection was inspired by the Renaissance and medieval folklore, but he added: "from my own state of mind too for the colors and the forms —I have tried to mix sport jackets and classical jackets, and this has nothing to do with retro."[69]

To keep the form of ancient clothes, but to forget their sense is something quite familiar in the Nineties. As long as there are more and more "historical" fashions, they have no more "historical" meanings. When the sense has not been completely forgotten, it has been somehow perverted. Far from meaning a return to the values of a historical period, most contemporary fashion creations mean all the contrary. For instance, Christian Lacroix's crinolines,

---

68. *Vogue*, France, February 1977.

69. *Vogue*, France, August 1981.

Vivienne Westwood's "faux culs," Jean-Paul Gaultier's, Thierry Mugler's, Alexander McQueen's, or John Galliano's corsets don't mean a restrained, dependent, and object-like woman, but are going in quite another direction. In his 1987 collection, Christian Lacroix's crinolines are actually mini-crinolines, and in being mini, they have something of the modernity of the Sixties and, consequently, they suggest a rather free and even dominant woman. Jean-Paul Gaultier's corsets are clearly ironical. The one he designed for Madonna, obviously, but also some others. While the traditional function of the corset was to show the breast by pushing it up, Jean-Paul Gaultier's corsets, on the contrary, crash it down and hide it.

When the Eighties or the Nineties fashion refers to the future, then this future is a way to express some of the Western fears. Thierry Mugler's cosmic inspiration gives an image of a somehow threatening femininity, incarnated by the Texan top model Jerry Hall and former Mick Jagger's wife, while it only presents, in the various advertisements promoting the brand, stereotyped and neuter science-fiction images in which verticality, steel, and glass dominate. The inspiration of other designers in the Nineties depicts a really fearful world to come and, consequently, betrays all the fears of our current societies. For instance, Jean-Paul Gaultier's "Mad Max" collection in the winter of 1995-1996, as well as Yohji Yamamoto's or Issey Miyake's post-nuclear, destructed, torn, dirty clothes. If Jean-Paul Gaultier was inspired by a famous movie of the

Eighties, the two Japanese designers seem to follow the American beat writer William Burroughs who, in 1969, had anticipated that the chic of the future could very well be made out of luxurious but torn and dirty clothes…

CHAPTER 4

SEXUAL IDENTITIES AND SEXUALITY

Against all odds - in any case, against all we were taught - fashion appears, as I have already tried to make it clear in the chapter above, as a very good tool for conducting sociological surveys, as well as a faithful reflection of the relations between the Western world and other civilizations on the one hand, and of the way the Western world relates to time and death on the other hand. Fashion images are portrayals of deep societal movements, but they can also initiate social changes. They are very important, indeed, in the contemporary redefinition of sexual identities, as well as in the new representations of sexuality. In these fields, I should even say that the part they play is a fundamental one. They have both sociological and psychological dimensions, which have seldom been closely studied, if, actually, they have been studied at all.

There is no doubt that the most obvious and visible characteristic of the last forty years in fashion is the reconsideration of what we may call the sexual dimorphism of the Western way of dressing. This way of dressing, which is based on the "opened system" for women and the "closed system" for men, was born in the Middle Ages and reinforced in the nineteenth century, where austerity was the rule for men, while only women had the right to wear color and indulge in some fantasy.

At the end of the Sixties, unisex fashion was definitely much more an ideal to reach than a concrete reality. And, as a conclusion to a collective work, *Men and Women: Dressing the Part*, Claudia Bush Kidwell puts it quite clearly: "No real androgynous clothes have ever existed for adults, men, and women."[70] But even if that statement is true, it is also the case that the clothing of men and women is much more similar today than it used to be. Even if their wardrobes resemble each other, one may say that the reason lies in the freedom of women to borrow many styles previously limited to men. Some anticipate that in the future, the "closed system" will dominate for both sexes, just as in Antiquity the "opened system" was the only system for men and women. But this is quite debatable. There is little doubt that it is quite difficult to find clothes once belonging to the men's wardrobe that do not belong today to the women's wardrobe (even some outerwear garments once regarded as typically masculine, such as the tie or the bow tie, can be seen on women), but the opposite is not as rare as we may think. There have been some attempts, to be sure very few, to introduce some "opened" styles in men's wardrobes: mainly some Eastern-like clothes such as djellabas in the Sixties or

---

70. C.B. Kidwell, "Conclusion" in *Men and Women: Dressing the Part* (ed. C.B. Kidwell and V. Steele), Washington D.C.: Smithsonian Institution Press, 1989, p. 158.

Jacques Esterel's masculine dresses in 1970, and, of course, more recently, Jean-Paul Gaultier's skirt. But the "opened system" is very far from having been adopted by men. On the other hand, many elements once reserved for women's clothes can be seen in men's clothing. Such elements include colors, fabrics, forms, and accessories. Thus, colors limited to women's garments in the nineteenth century can be seen on men's shirts and may even extend to trousers and jackets. The latter, for example, are no longer just black, gray, or dark blue as in the bourgeois societies of the nineteenth century. The fabrics (silk or satin, for instance) or the forms that were those of women's clothes have also become those of men's clothes. As for jewels, once reserved exclusively for women, they too began to be worn on men's necks and wrists with the advent of the hippy movement. We may even interpret the disappearance of the tie, man's best identification, as a step towards femininity. That may not have been obvious with Pierre Cardin's Mao collar jacket, but in showing man's neck and torso or in playing on the sensuousness of an open collar, Gianni Versace had a model: the feminine décolleté, as he said in his book, *Men without Ties.*[71]

Anyhow, the growing similarities between men's and women's clothes are not without consequences. As the clothing of men and women becomes more similar, the differences between masculine and feminine roles narrow as well. The

---

71. G. Versace, *Men without Ties*, New York, Paris, London: Abbeville Press, 1997.

annexation by women of men's clothes determines the annexation of roles once reserved for men. It has been said that the dress or the skirt was the outfit that defined the place of women in society and kept them away from any other activity but motherhood. Consequently, and quite logically, pants for women should free them both physically and psychologically from all of the restraints, so that they could live, to quote a well-known French sociologist, "without keeping the knees close to each other" and get involved in activities that were refused to them before: commercial activities, sports, and so on. But beyond social roles, strictly speaking, the change in clothes also modified feminine identity in general.

If we consider that the feminine identity is a question of coherence between the way a woman sees herself (self-perception), and the way she appears to others (representation and the way others show her as a woman), we can understand the fundamental role that clothes play in this building up of identity, for clothes stand on the borderline between interiority and exteriority.[72]

Therefore, some will say that clothes are a feminine more than a masculine question, as illustrated, for instance, quite well how difficult it is for a woman to make up her mind between different clothes in any circumstance. One will also say that this feminine dimension of clothes is the very proof of a more particular sensitivity to identity on the woman's side

---

72. See N. Heinich, *Etats de femme. L'Identité féminine dans la fiction occidentale*, Paris: Gallimard, 1996, p. 333.

than on the man's side. It may be. But if the identity function of clothes is less important and dramatic for men than for women, it does not mean that this function does not exist for men as well. There is no doubt that fashion, for at least the last thirty years, has brought about changes in masculine identity as well as in feminine identity (masculine identity which is definitely far more fluid than is commonly thought)[73] or at least has revealed some previously unacknowledged characteristics of masculine identity.

If clothing styles suggest a reconsideration of sexual roles with the entry of women into what was identified as men's fields and, to an extent, the insertion of feminine values into the masculine universe, the sexual identities defined by clothes are nevertheless far from aiming at androgyny. On the contrary, the situation is far more complicated than Yves Saint Laurent thought it was when, in the Seventies, he pointed out: "I am interested in ambiguity; that is life because men dress as women and women as men. They all wear the same clothes today."

But let us go a little bit further.

What is revealed at first through the feminization of men's clothes is the feminine essence of a certain way of being a man, while the masculinization of women's clothes is very often just another way to be feminine.

---

73. See H. Amigorena/F. Monneyron (ed.), *Le Masculin. Fictions, identité, dissémination*, Paris: L'Harmattan, 1998.

What is revealed in the men's use of some elements from the women's clothes is the active principle of masculine seduction. As I have pointed out in one of my most well-known books,[74] to seduce a man, is clearly to engage in feminine strategies; that is to say, every technique leading to masculine seduction involves some feminine elements. In the eighteenth century, it was mainly in the tactics of seduction of such great seducers as Lovelace, Valmont, or Casanova that we can read about this effemination. But, if in the nineteenth century, the dandy proved to be a seductive figure, that is because he incorporated in his own body, by means of the clothes, or by the care he has for his own appearance, something of the feminine essence. And, again, in the Sixties and Seventies, what is revealed through the feminization of men's clothes even more dramatically and, at least, on a larger social scale is the feminine dimension that colors what masculine seduction is made of. Such a dimension was well illustrated by the photograph of Jim Morrison arrayed in Gloria Stavers' furs in 1969, or by Mick Jagger in his party dress at the Hyde Park concert in 1969, or by actors such as Terence Stamp and Helmut Berger portrayed in unisex tunics for Yves Saint Laurent. Consequently, man is more and more attracted to the field of beauty and is transformed from being a subject of desire to becoming an object of desire – to the point that Jean-Paul Gaultier viewed the new millennium as

---

74. F. Monneyron, *Séduire. L'Imaginaire de la séduction de Don Giovanni à Mick Jagger*, Paris: PUF, 1997.

the era of the male as sex object. This effeminate man is indeed an object of heterosexual desire as a seductive figure for women, but he is also an object of homosexual desire, for the Western representations have made of effeminization, roughly at the end of the nineteenth century, a sign of male homosexuality. Consequently, the new masculine identity which was just being created as a result of changes in menswear in the Sixties and Seventies is an identity in which bisexuality appears as a normal form of sexuality. David Bowie was quite illustrative of this development. At the beginning of the seventies, he borrowed women's clothes and accessories and was photographed in a woman's dress for one of his records. His next step was a declaration of his bisexuality.

In 1969, Yves Saint Laurent used to say: "I want to find for women an equivalent uniform to a man's suit." We all know that this uniform has been the skirt suit, already invented by Coco Chanel, but Yves Saint Laurent made it even more popular, to such a point that in the early Eighties one says a "Saint Laurent" instead of a "skirt suit." This woman's outfit, made out of the dry materials used for men's suits, has the same functions as the latter. But it is not a loss of femininity. It is even, for most people, the most feminine outerwear you can ever imagine, even more so when it has as a complement a blouse, the Yves Saint Laurent "see-through blouse" or any other kind of blouse. However, the skirt suit is far from defining a masculine gender or even a masculine-feminine gender between which the executive woman would hesitate, and she needs not to wear additional silk stockings to keep her femininity alive, for it is pure femininity in itself, and it may be the most perfect sign of femininity. In opposition to this skirt suit, the pantsuit or the tuxedo clearly belongs to the "closed system" of men's clothes. But when worn by women, such attire suggests absolute femininity. Yves Saint Laurent, who, even more than the skirt suit, initiated the tux and the pantsuit for women at the end of the Sixties, pointed out that "pants are not a sign of equality but another charm for women; a woman in a pantsuit is very far from being masculine". With the passing of time, this super-femininity of the woman's body in masculine clothes has become quite obvious. The femininity of Giorgio Armani's masculine-feminine suit has been praised throughout the Western world in advertising campaigns and movies. And this suit has become the common outerwear for executive women of the Eighties and the Nineties.

As we see, what we may interpret as a trend towards androgyny could not actually get rid of the physical sexes. To a certain extent, we could even say that the sexes do use this trend towards androgyny to their benefit. However, the feminization of men's clothes and the masculinization of women's clothes are not the only definitions of masculine and feminine identities.

For two decades or so, clothes have defined a new representation and, accordingly, a new social identity of male homosexuality. Homosexuality was regarded since the end of the nineteenth century as an inversion (that was even the medical term used at the time), and the physical feminization of the clothes was its main representation. Today, this representation is still valid, but another and quite opposite representation has developed. Nowadays, homosexuality is also proclaimed by styles of clothing that have a very manly connotation. Leather clothes, which identified some decades ago the gays from San Francisco or from any other homosexual community in the States or in Europe, and which, once reconsidered by designers such as Gianni Versace, define today the homosexual universe as a universe of pure manhood, with no feminine references at all. In recent years, a similar fashion can be found in the Marais, the homosexual area in Paris, which is fond of military clothes: battle-dress pants and accessories, revealing tee-shirts, and tight sleeveless turtleneck sweaters, etc. If this "homosexual" fashion, once it has been reworked by designers, was quite a success among a very large range of heterosexual buyers, it has even changed the image of the homosexual, no longer an image of a "third sex" but the image of the pure male.

Female identity is definitely firmer than male identity. If some rather shallow books have tried to assert the opposite, a sociological approach to clothes makes it quite clear. Indeed, the fashion images are very often traditional images of women. They come from the old myths and are re-adapted to the conditions of our modernity or post-modernity. They define a woman's identity little altered by social changes. They are always idealized or derogatory images of females, coming from very different periods.

Let us begin with the Sixties. Except for trousers that allow women to assume the social roles of men, without, as we have seen, questioning a woman's identity, the main outerwear of the Sixties is the miniskirt. And there is no doubt that the miniskirt offers two different images of women: an image of purity and innocence and an image of sexuality. Indeed, the miniskirt is the transposition on adult women of children's clothes and, consequently, it transfers to women the characteristics of childhood: purity, innocence, and even virginity. But this angel-like vision does not last long. As the miniskirt plays with the veiled-unveiled scheme, according to some psychoanalysts, the measure of man's desire, the woman who wears it is sexually attractive and soon a temptress, the one who dominates men by means of sexuality, and even approximates the role of a prostitute. As an outer garment, the miniskirt has indeed changed. The first miniskirts to be seen in André Courrèges' collections were actually mini-dresses (not so mini, by the way) worn with socks or with small sock-like boots, and, accordingly, they resembled baby-doll style, while, later on, miniskirts were shorter and closer to the skin, far more suggestive, and, once emancipated from the children's outerwear, they became the garments of an emancipated woman, self-assured and very conscious of her sex appeal.

The fashion of the Seventies also proposes these two images of women, not in a succession this time but rather in a juxtaposition. In the early Seventies, a longer skirt comes back, and, with it, if not the image of an asexual or virginal woman, then probably an image of a more respectable woman. Actually, it could even be a provocative image when the long skirt is opened up high on the thighs – or to the waist, as in an evening dress by Yves Saint Laurent in 1970. The same thing is true with respect to the ethnic style of the early Seventies initiated by Kenzo, which soon had a large number of followers and an enduring impact during most of the decade. While proposing a very natural and candid image of the female, the Indian ponchos, the Afghan jackets, and the Romanian blouses, later on, the "retro" skirts and blouses also propose the image of a seductive woman, for all these clothes suggest a total freedom, a freedom in the way of getting dressed as well as of one's body. Yves Saint Laurent, thinking of the Seventies, said in 1986: "Women, at that time, had a very special seduction (...) They had never been, in the movies, in the photographs, so attractive. Because they looked free and happy. Maybe because they were waiting for marvelous things to come and there were lights in their eyes. All that made them click their high heels on the sidewalks and, joyfully, they rediscovered silk, colors, the pleasure of getting dressed, the pleasure of seduction. They did not care about fashion. Nor did I."

The fashion of the Eighties built up yet another image of a woman, an incarnation of sexuality who is quite conscious of how attractive she is to men. This image began to take shape at the end of the Seventies with Yves Saint Laurent's Russian and Chinese collections, portraying women as cruel goddesses, femmes fatales, or girls from the harem, while stockings and high heels made a comeback on the streets. Thierry Mugler, drawing inspiration from comic strips, science fiction, and Hollywood movies of the Forties and Fifties, played a significant role in shaping this image of women. His fashion portrays a dominant and dangerous female, reflecting perhaps some masculine fears regarding women's increasingly visible roles in social and economic life. If the skirt suit, blending feminine seduction with masculine functionality, is somewhat ambiguous, Thierry Mugler intensified it. With his skirt suits, especially his "tailleurs trotteurs", he presents a very structured look with wide padded shoulders and narrow skirts, embodying a woman who is both highly attractive and self-assured. As one commentator noted: "Spacegirl or rodeogirl, kolkozgirl or Vampirella, Blue Angel, Lady Mugler is always a kind of Gradiva who reads Freud, comic strips, and *Dangerous Liaisons*".

These femme fatale images will still be present in the fashion of the early Nineties, as in collections by Alaia and Versace, and even in some of Christian

Lacroix's collections. But in this last decade, the feminine identity has become very elusive; there are no dominant female images. *Vogue*, at least in the French edition, has renounced any kind of quintessence and just enumerates the different options: mini, long, masculine-feminine, leather, large, colored, black, etc. It is a very good indication that there is no dominant feminine image with which women could identify. At best, some traditional or new woman roles, and the identities that come from them, are put side by side, such as in *Vogue*, September 1998. There can be found the traditional "femme-maîtresse (woman as mistress)," very sexy, in leather, short skirt, high stiletto heels, to whom are opposed two women far less sexy, almost asexual: the "maîtresse-femme (woman as master)" who is "triumphant in the men's world thanks to her mind and intelligence" and who wears clothes such as a coat-dress in gabardine but doubled with chiffon, or "la femme égale de l'homme (the equal-to-man woman)" who hesitates between skirt suit and pants suit, between seduction with lace and silk or business with an old-time shirt.

Fashion images are quite essential in the expression of feminine and masculine identities but also in the building up and in the definition and redefinition of these identities. However, that is not their only function. They also give us a very good picture of the relation to sexuality in one historical period and, consequently, they may help to understand this period.

We can read in clothes our aspirations as well as our fears related to sexuality. Clothes express, says Jean-Paul Gaultier, and he is right in saying that, "the importance of sexuality in our life." Therefore, the history of fashion is the history of our relation to sexuality.

Even if, as I pointed out in my book on seduction, seduction and sexuality are two different worlds that are governed by different laws, it is true, nevertheless, that sexual experience is linked to the ability to seduce. In our desires to seduce, there is little doubt that clothes play a very important part, for they appear to help seduction. Consequently, clothes are a very reliable means to know how one sees and lives one's sexuality.

"The word seduction is taking over the word elegance. That is a way of living rather than a way of getting dressed," Yves Saint Laurent said in the late 1960s. This shift from a codified elegance with its rules and social restraints to a freer seduction that only obeys the mysterious laws of desire is quite significant. As the British fashion journalist Catherine Storr puts it, this shift anticipated women's liberation at the clothing level and, accordingly, helped them to have a freer sexuality. Indeed, Sixties fashion, as well as Seventies fashion, determined a way of living and, at first, a freer and more spontaneous way of living one's sexuality. The fashion of these two decades has multiplied, mainly for women, the possibilities of choice between different types of clothes, and this is already an affirmation of freedom and, symbolically, being open to all experiences. But, most of all, they are the ultimate step of a very important change that began fifty years before.

During the nineteenth century, the female body was hidden under layers of dresses, and from the Twenties began an important change that showed more and more nudity and natural forms, so feminine attractiveness was no longer linked to modesty. No doubt that this change was accelerated in the Sixties. Some very important inventions, such as the miniskirt and see-through clothes, on the one hand, and jeans, on the other hand, were a great revolution. And this revolution in clothes also means a revolution in ethics. A body that flaunts itself, after being hidden, develops a new relation to sexuality, a relation to a sexuality that is now seen as an affirmation of life. We know that these inventions proved to be scandalous to some people, and to others, on the contrary, they were seen as the true symbols of revolt: for instance, Yves Saint Laurent's see-through blouses were scandalous to America, while some designers stressed the erotic side of the miniskirt or the jeans. These different positions clearly show that the revolution in clothes was also a revolution in ethics.

This sexual liberation is to be seen again in the Seventies fashion, with some differences. Nudity and close-to-the-skin clothes are still important in the fashion of this new decade, but some other elements belonging to the past are there again. Thus, at the end of the Seventies, while see-through clothes and close-to-the-skin clothes are on any woman, high heels, for instance, can be seen again. They had not completely disappeared but belonged to a special world –the world of prostitution. Anyway, to wear high heels changes the way a woman walks and her general appearance. A lot of the natural movements of the body are amplified, and the sex appeal of the person, consequently, is possibly increased. Most generally, in making the figure taller, it also provides some elegance. To many people, men or women, high heels are a symbol of femininity, and, as they give women elegance, they are also the sign of a refined sexuality that hesitates between domination and subjection. In adding this traditional element of seduction and some others to a nudity regarded as naturally attractive, the Eighties fashion still suggests a free sexuality but with a touch of perversity, perversions such as sadism and masochism being then just the ultimate transgression, as in Helmut Newton's photographs.

Fashion, from the Nineties on, expresses quite a different relation to sexuality. Some sexual perversions are still expressed by it, but the general trend has nothing to do with sexual freedom. Indeed, the fashion of the Nineties is the very best expression of a new social imaginary entirely reconsidered by the AIDS epidemic, and the general atmosphere is anti-seduction and anti-sexuality.

This evolution can be seen firstly in the economic evolution. The desire to seduce is also a desire to consume. It drives one to buy what can be a tool for seduction, in particular to buy clothes that may enhance one's attractiveness or hide some disadvantages. In the Western world during the last few decades, fashion industries have been rather in financial straits. In France, there was an 8% decline in clothing expenses. This could mean that we don't want to seduce anymore. But fashion itself shows that no one wants to consume. If the very essence of fashion is to never last, in order to always be renewed, the fashion of the Nineties and Two thousands was a non-fashion: both a refusal to seduce and to consume, as Grunge is a good example. Grunge hides the body with old clothes and refuses the very idea of elegance and seduction.

Some clothes of contemporary designers are very illustrative of this trend. Vivienne Westwood's creations could be very good examples, but I shall stress some other ones,such as the black coat dresses by Rei Kawakubo that entirely hide the body and the monk-inspired style that we find in the clothes of the Japanese designers as well as in those of some European designers. The ultimate step is doubtlessly the attempt by the Belgian designer Martin Margiela to deconstruct fashion by exposing all the inside construction of his creations. Such an attempt means a deconstruction of what clothes signify: seduction and sexuality.

This itinerary of the (mainly) female clothing that goes from the Sixties and Seventies seduction to its refusal in the Nineties is also the underwear itinerary. Even better, underwear, and especially female underwear, that "exploits all the resources of the imaginary" and illustrates "a sensuous semantics"[75] is to be regarded as a perfect and illustrative summary.

Dropping bras aimed at the feminist movements to free the female body from all of its constraints did not free this body from male desire. On the contrary, caught in the veiled-unveiled, the founding dialectics of male desire, and intensified by close-fitting clothes and transparencies, it has an important erotic power and suggests a free sexuality to be expressed spontaneously. Pantyhose worn under the miniskirt is part of that same dialectic, more indirectly. Incidentally, the reappearance in the late seventies of stockings and garter belts that had been replaced by pantyhose, far from being as paradoxical as some think, belongs to the same logic of the symbolic representation of sexuality. That this reappearance proves concomitant with the creation of the string that only hides the essential is already quite significant. It simply manifests another seduction that plays more with the artificial than with the natural. In this respect, it is twice inscribed in the veiled-unveiled dialectics: in itself, since the stockings drive the eyes along the leg towards the sex framed by the garter belt, and since the flesh and the fabrics alternate (with even more strength when the latter is black and contrasts with the white skin). And in allowing a new hesitation since, as Jacques Laurent noticed in 1978, "twenty years ago a woman was wearing innocently and naturally a garter belt under

---

75. C. Saint-Laurent (J. Laurent), *Histoire imprévus des dessous féminins*, Paris: Herscher, 1986.

her skirt; today she is aware that this attitude means something, for her and for the other."[76]

In the Eighties, this erotic dimension of underwear was broken. The reintroduction of the old corset or its transformation into beautiful outerwear could still be interpreted as partaking of the sexual logic, but underwear worn as outerwear or over clothes is no longer seductive. When announced in the early Eighties by Alaïa, Gaultier, and Chanel and generalized in the mid-Eighties ("Les dessous se dévoilent et prennent le dessus/Underwear goes outwear," pointed out French *Vogue* in February 1995).[77] This utilization can be regarded as breaking the last sexual taboos,[78] with it, desire is broken too, without even referring to the idea that desire is being fed by what is forbidden. Desire is destroyed when the public and the private are confused. "Mysterious clothes, since they are destined to be worn in the mystery of their dissimulation."[79] Lingerie holds its erotic allure when only visible in intimacy; it promises sexual activity. When taken out of intimacy, it loses this drive. Even masculine underwear, traditionally "governed by a sense not far from indifference,"[80] but that has been somehow eroticized by Calvin Klein's skillful advertising campaigns in the Eighties, is subjected to this sexual disinvestment when

---

76. J. Laurent, *Le Nu vêtu et dévêtu*, Paris: Gallimard-Idées, 1979, p. 163.

77. *Vogue*, France, February 1995, p. 41.

78. V. Steele, *Fetish. Fashion, sex and power*, p. 133.

79. M. Toussaint-Samat, op.cit., p. 385.

80. C. Saint Laurent, *op. cit.*

it becomes apparent or is worn as outerwear. Firstly limited to some poor neighborhood teenagers, the fashion that lets trunks be seen over the jeans has reached the catwalks and then a larger number of men, while some other underwear, such as the working-class tank top, is to be exhibited as well. That Yves Saint Laurent's menswear has gone that way too, advertising it under the open shirt of a man in a photo shoot is significant of vulgarity, for it is vulgarity in every sense of the word.

To keep oneself out of desire and sexuality, as has been expressed by the fashion of the last decade, is underlined, if not so directly but as significantly, by some directions of today's clothing creation. An ongoing fascination for some specific materials is a first example. No one could deny that the AIDS epidemic is certainly one of the main causes of beauty and desire becoming suspect and, consequently, of the societal uneasiness introduced by this suspicion. And that more and more clothes, especially close-fitting jumpsuits, are made, as condoms, out of latex - as it is frequently noted - appears as a metaphor for the physical constraints weighing on sexuality and the absence of spontaneity they lead to. A second example is the passing in the fashion universe of an ensemble of diverse sexual perversions, from fetishism to sadomasochism, with fashion designers like Gaultier or Versace being inspired by them. If, in the late Seventies, the Punks had already brought this ensemble out of the boudoirs, private rooms, and pornographic films in which they were maintained,[81] while a fashion photographer like Helmut Newton gives it some legitimacy, it only reached Haute Couture and the high street in the Nineties. This passing has to be regarded as a compensation in the fashion images for the uneasiness of that period vis-à-vis desire and sexuality.

Fetishism, as it is interpreted by Freud in *Drei Abhandlungen zur Sexualtheorie (Three Essays on the Theory of Sexuality)*, is, indeed, a metonymy that substitutes for the object of desire a part of the body or a piece of clothing before idealizing them.[82] Without this displacement being felt as painful.[83] In these last years, an increase in lingerie sales could be seen as a testimony to a collective fetishism that could be grounded even more in the contemporary fashion interest in leather and underwear. This excessive and often thrilling interest does appear as the displacement, carried out by a whole society through a designer, of a desire that cannot and does not want to be normally, or perversely, expressed in the reality of life, on a material connoting sexuality or on a piece of fabric announcing it, as Freud was able to identify for one of his patients but, here, for a whole society. The older pieces of lingerie are, indeed, the most significant. For these pieces stage a displacement all the more important as it is not only a displacement between two ontological levels (imaginary and reality) but a historical displacement. In this respect,

---

81 . D. Hebdidge, *Subculture. The Meaning of Style*, London: Routledge, 1993.

82. S. Freud, *Drei Abhandlungen zur Sexualtheorie*, Frankfurt am Main: Fischer, 1996 (1st ed. 1905).

83. S. Freud, *Zur Genese des Fetischismus, op. cit.*

the interest in the corset, already analyzed in a chapter above, is to be kept in mind, particularly if this underwear, as the latex jumpsuit, is to be regarded as a metaphor for the constriction the AIDS imaginary has helped to set.

When fetishism can be read as euphemizing desire, it is rather dramatization that has to be read in other perversions that are represented, directly or indirectly, by the most recent fashion images. One can understand that, at the time in which desire, judged as dangerous, is becoming suspect, and at a time in which norms, or at least constraining social representations, weigh on sexuality, in return, what is forbidden is even more eroticized. As the sexual drive, which is also a life drive, cannot blossom, it tends to transmute, says Freud, into a death drive directed towards the object or the subject of desire.[84] But now, it does appear sublimated, in the fashion world, as a figure of sadism and masochism. A flurry of designers—coming from the Punk movement,such as Vivienne Westwood, Betsey Johnson, and others—use sadomasochist themes, but the best example is indisputably Gianni Versace in 1992 with his *Bondage* collection, summarizing and intensifying trends already present in the creations of Claude Montana and Thierry Mugler,[85]

---

84. S. Freud, *Das Unbehagen in der Kultur (Civilization and its Discontents), Frankfurt am Main: Fischer, 2009* (1st ed. 1930).

85. The former was known for his sexy leather outfits and has dressed women with studded leather jackets while the latter went even further with a metal bustier that transforms women in biker-like figure.

the Italian designer presents a whole collection of clothes, mostly in leather, clearly associated with "radical" sexuality such as sadism and masochism. This collection, depicted in photographs where women are either holding a whip or are harnessed and ridden with a leash or a dog collar, has been disputed by feminists. They wonder whether Versace, who has declared that to get liberated, women had to have the right to be sexually aggressive, was magnifying them or degrading them. But the most important aspect lies elsewhere. As V. Steele has made it clear.[86] Women's liberation was not so much the question, but rather a rebel, hedonist, powerful, and provocative sexuality; it could also be added that there is a sublimated and virtual sexuality.

---

86. V. Steele, *Fetish*, p. 161.

CHAPTER 5

SOCIETIES

The sociological approach encouraged by fashion images can be developed even more. Fashion images reveal, as we have seen, the main orientations of society as far as its relations to other civilizations, on the one hand, and its relations to sexuality, on the other hand, are concerned. And these results are indeed incentive to go even further. Accordingly, if we can provide ourselves with the adequate methodological tools, fashion images are a very good way to penetrate, under the social surface, into the societal depths and to find out the schemas, the archetypes, and the main anthropological structures which define a period and give it sense. Fashion images consequently make it possible to identify the main moments of the sociocultural dynamics in the Western world if we stick to the very same period that has previously been studied.

We can conduct this research with the methodological tools provided by Gilbert Durand's anthropological theories regarding images and symbols. To an extent, fashion images, which have the repressed

Mundus Imaginalis main functions, could even be regarded as a very good training field for G. Durand's methods, and even as a confirmation of their validity.

Gilbert Durand considers that the human imagination always and mainly represents, figures and symbolizes time and death, to reduce the anguish linked to our experience of time. Consequently, aside from creating images of time and images of death, the function of imagination is a function of euphemization, but far from being something negative, a mask hung up before the ugly figure of death, it should be regarded, on the contrary, as something dynamic and prospective, that tends to improve the situation of the human being in the world.[87] In *Les structures anthropologiques de l'imaginaire (The Anthropological Structures of the Imaginary)*, he points out that our symbolic representations are linked to our body gestures and the nerves. Focusing on works in reflexology, he distinguishes three main "dominant reflexes": the postural one, the digestive one, and the sexual one[88] and he says that the symbolic representations are indeed determined by these "dominant reflexes." All that is luminous and visual, as well as the techniques of separation and purification, of which the weapons, arrows, and swords particularly are frequent symbols, are determined by the postural reflex. Everything that has a relation with depth, such as water or earth, and stimulates something that contains, such

---

87. G. Durand, *L'Imagination symbolique, op. cit.*, p. 118.

88. G. Durand, *Les structures anthropologiques de l'imaginaire*, Paris: Dunod, 1984 (1st ed. 1960), p. 47.

as cups or coffers, and, consequently, is an incentive to the technical dreams of drinking and food, is determined by the digestive reflex. The seasonal rhythms and all the technical substitutes of the cycle, such as the wheel and the spinning wheel, are determined by the sexual reflex.[89] The images created by human imagination can be sorted into three main "structural ways": the heroic structures that are part of the diurnal order of the image, the mystic structures, and the synthetic structures which partake of the nocturnal order. The heroic structures can be expressed through the symbolism of elevation, light, and fight. The first heroic structure can be represented by the pragmatic deficit. The second one by the *Spaltung*, the fact of separating one thing from another. The third one by the geometrization, and the fourth one by the antithesis.[90] The mystic structures can be expressed through the symbolism of descent, intimacy, and crouching. The first one is characterized by duplication, the second one by the viscosity of the representative elements, the third one by the sensuality of the representations, and the fourth one by minuteness and miniaturization.[91] The synthetic structures and the other intentions of imagination[92] are expressed by the symbolism of cycle and progress. The first one is characterized by the harmonization of the contraries.

---

89. *Ibid.* p. 55

90. *Ibid.,* p. 209.

91. *Ibid.,* p. 308

92. *Ibid.,* p. 399.

The second one by dialectics. The third one by history. The fourth one by progress.[93].

Since the totality of the images can be hosted in these three general structures, these structures are relevant for any imaginary creation. Notwithstanding, it may prove useful to adapt their characteristics to a particular object, namely to transfer them to the specific field of clothes and fashion.

The fabrics, cut, draped, or sewn, become an image once they are worn by someone. It is not by chance that fashion magazines sell and promote clothes with the help of models. The fashion runway shows are an extension of this habit.[94] But even if it is true that clothes do not exist and do not become images but on a body, it is interesting, as an experiment, to distinguish images created only by the clothes themselves from the fashion images which imply a model and even a photographic scenery.

The visual impressions that come from the form, the color, the motifs of clothes, to which could be added different accessories such as bags, hats, shoes, or jewels, can already be interpreted as images and, consequently, be classified in the structural categories defined by Gilbert Durand.

We can consider that clothes belonging to the diurnal order and to the heroic structures have, one way or another, some symbolic link with time and death. We can mention black clothes that, in the Western

---

93. *Ibid.*, p. 400.

94. See F. Borel, *Le Vêtement incarné. Les métamorphoses du corps*, Paris: Calmann-Lévy, 1992, p. 55.

symbolism of clothing, are associated with mourning, but it is also true for any outfit and accessory made out of animal skin, such as a fur coat or crocodile shoes, which call upon a theriomorphic symbolism, significant of the primal fears of human beings. In the heroic structures of the diurnal order, but this time as an antithesis of death, we can classify every huge outerwear, large ceremonial clothes, for instance, or any outerwear that bears constraint on the body, both inconvenient to wear and a good example of the pragmatic deficit. In the same structures, we can also classify clothes that play on the opposition veiled/unveiled, such as the miniskirt or, in general, any outerwear that, with its form and motifs (stripes, for example), is somehow geometrical.

Similarly, we can consider the characteristics of the mystical structures of the nocturnal order: a desire for union and a taste for secret intimacy[95] can also be related to these structures the colored fabrics, since G. Durand considers that in the nocturnal order all the colors are represented, while in the so-called diurnal order a black and white dialectic is to be found.[96] Slightly more difficult is the identification of clothes that belong to the synthetic structures of the nocturnal order. But we can very well admit that all the clothes that offer a synthesis of the opposites or are in a dialectical relation belong to these synthetic structures. If we take as an example the masculine/feminine

---

95. G. Durand, *Les structures anthropologiques de l'imaginaire*, p. 308.

96. *Ibid.*, p. 250.

opposition, based on the open/closed opposition, we can consider, indeed, that every outwear that tends to abolish it belongs to the synthetic structures. Opposing and then harmonizing clothes that come from two different cultural traditions, Western and Eastern, for instance, could be considered as belonging to the synthetic structures too. At last, calling in ancient clothes to institute a relation between past and present, or imagining what clothes could be in the future, are good examples of the two synthetic structures of history and progress.

All the above relations can be gathered in the following table.

	Diurnal	Order	Nocturnal	Order
	Visions of time	Heroic Structures	Mystic Structures	Synthetic Structures
Form		- Pragmatic deficit -Antithesis -Geometry	-Duplication -Superposition -Draperies -Pleats	-Harmonization of the contraries, dialectics (masculine/femini ne, West/East) -History
Color	Black	Clear/Dar k	All the colors	Opposition/Harm onization of Colors
Material	Animal Skin	Leather, metallic material	Latex, synthetic material (viscosity), wool (sensuousness)	
Motifs	Animal motifs	Stripes, squares	Embroideries, prints	Circles, Crosses

This table needs to be commented upon. One may object that if a particular piece of clothing can be interpreted in terms of heroic structures as long as its form is concerned, it could be interpreted in terms of mystic structures as long as its color, fabrics, or prints are concerned. This objection, which is not specific to clothing images but is also valid for any kind of images, is not as fundamental as one may think. On the one hand, form, color, fabrics, and prints are not so much in opposition as we may fear they are, as if the designers' imagination were unable to juxtapose different structures. On the other hand, there is always a dominant element that determines the image, generally the very form of clothing.

Another objection is actually more important; it turns out to be a diachronic argument about the history and evolution of clothes. A particular piece of clothing can very well be interpreted as belonging to specific structures (heroic, synthetic, or mystic) when it first appears and develops in the fashion world, and later on, this interpretation will no longer stand. For instance, the pantsuit for women, which questioned, in the Sixties, the dimorphism of the Western clothing system, had to be regarded at that time as belonging to the synthetic structures. However, today, when all the designers are making pantsuits, they are actually no longer significant of these structures. Over the past twenty years, women's wardrobes have been greatly extended, so that the designers, in most of their collections, present any possible forms: dresses, skirts, pants; long, short, large, slim, etc. Consequently, the form can no longer be considered the relevant and dominant element but has to be replaced, or at least duplicated, with other elements: color, fabrics, or prints. If the miniskirt, for instance, can be interpreted, without any hesitation, within the Sixties context as belonging to the heroic structures, to be related to the same structures in the Nineties and Two Thousand context, it has to be black and made out of leather. On the contrary, in the Nineties and Two Thousands, pantsuits with embroideries, prints, and bright colors would not be interpreted as belonging to the synthetic structures but rather to the mystic structures. It is worth noticing, indeed, that some fashion magazines tend to interpret their own classification in terms of structures, as did *L'Officiel* in August 1999, for the "Medieval Orthodox," described as "synthetic structures."[97]

Accordingly, the different elements have to be crossed, so that the structures of the clothing imaginary can be properly identified. But, obviously, other elements have to be taken into account, exterior elements to clothes so to speak. We have to introduce the ones who wear clothes and how they wear them, that is to say, the fashion model and the photographic context, which have been forgotten so far, but could be of great help. In short, we have to consider the imaginary of fashion and no more the imaginary of clothes.

---

97. *L'Officiel*, Supplément, August 1999, p. 5.

With a specific model and a specific scenario, the images of fashion do introduce, in particular, images of time and death. Along with black color and animal prints, there is little doubt that a model such as the blonde Jerry Hall has embodied for Thierry Mugler this deathly and fearful femininity that the designer in the Eighties had pictured in many of his advertising campaigns. But the fashion images are revealing, sometimes quite independently of the clothes they are promoting, heroic, mystic, or synthetic structures. If we stick to Thierry Mugler, we can notice that the photographs promoting his brand are always organized around ascension or verticality symbols (skyscrapers, steep mountains, etc.) or around separation or cutting symbols (metallic objects, glass material, etc.), all belonging to the heroic structures. Conversely, a lot of photographs can be found that duplicate or determine the mystic structures of clothes, offering an aquatic element, as seen in a series in the Italian March 1999 *Vogue* titled "Floating," or playing with different symbols of intimacy.

When we work our way out with these methodological principles, a large body of fashion images can be studied quite rigorously. And focusing on *Vogue* for forty years or more, we can, therefore, identify the main trends that are significant of our society's subterranean aspirations and fears in a particular period of time. Obviously, only trends can be identified because the fashion images issued from the collections of a season or a year, even if they have been selected by a fashion magazine such as *Vogue,* do not all belong to one and only structure of the imaginary. But it may sound fair and reasonable to say that a trend can be identified in a particular time period when at least 70% of the images belong to the very same structures.

The fashion images created during the 1965-1970 period (both in Haute Couture and ready-to-wear) largely belong to the diurnal order and the heroic structures. Eighty percent of the images that have been analyzed in *Vogue* belong to a heroic universe, while the remaining twenty percent of images, in equal shares, are mystic or synthetic. If we consider the clothes themselves, the model who wears them, or the context in which they are worn, the heroic elements are extremely dominant. We can take, for example, a very significant French *Vogue* photo-shoot in August 1966. This photo-shoot presents clothes with straight forms and geometrical prints worn by an ethereal model whose feet do not even touch the ground, while, in the background, Wall Street skyscrapers can be seen, a good illustration of verticality. Aside from the representation of a fatal femininity portrayed in a model clad in a long black dress, photographed on the Coney Island seaside walk, or the theriomorphic symbols that are panther fur coats from Somalia or Abyssinia.[98] The symbols linked to the heroic structures are dominant. We have the spectacular and diaretic symbols that we can find with the clothes and the models on one hand, and the

---

98. *Vogue,* France, September 1967.

ascension symbols of the photographic scenery on the other hand. Consequently, the figures of separation, antithesis, or geometry, dominant in the clothes and the fashion images, can be interpreted as a Promethean aspiration with an important pragmatic deficit. The miniskirts that play with the antithesis veiled/unveiled, the dresses with geometrical motifs, the stripes, and the black and white square prints, the metallic elements, and the leather boots —all these are, as we know, the main outfits and identifiers of this period, with solar blonde models who come, at that time, very often from Scandinavia and pose in a scenery where verticality, gigantism, sky, space, light, and sun are the main elements. Some collections, of course, are very illustrative of these heroic structures: the winter 1965 "Mondrian" collection by Yves Saint Laurent with its rigorous symmetries, Pierre Cardin's mini dresses collection for Spring 1968, André Courrèges' spatial suits, and Paco Rabanne's metallic dresses. Some fashion photographs are also very illustrative, such as Veruschka's by Franco Rubartelli, with Veruschka posing as a hunter with the African bush in the background for Yves Saint Laurent's safari jacket, or Maud Betelsen's by Gunnar Larsen, in the mountain ski resort Les Diablerets, with the blue sky and the mountains in the background, very hieratic in a metallic dress and headdress by Paco Rabanne.

If the fashion images that can be related to the nocturnal order of the image are rarer in the Sixties, there are still 20% of them, and these 20% of images did actually determine how the images of the following decade looked. Clothes that were to be found in the Sixties, the trousers for women that were to be interpreted as a good example of the harmonization of the contraries, part of the synthetic structures, as well as pleated skirts or ruffled dresses, significant of the mystic structures, are elements that determined the main directions of the next decade. Conversely, the Seventies fashion images show some heroic elements, resurgences from the previous decade.

Indeed, if some heroic elements are still to be identified in the 1970 and 1971 creations, they disappear soon after in favor of other elements belonging to the mystic and synthetic structures. Miniskirts, or what may appear as a reconsideration of them, the long slit skirt,[99] geometric clothes, stripes, square prints, and leather are very quickly replaced by maxi skirts, long dresses, and pantsuits; by flowered prints, incrustations, embroideries, duplications, juxtapositions; and by a larger number of colors.

To a large extent, the Seventies fashion images can be interpreted as a total immersion in the nocturnal order, and these images are an equal share between synthetic structures and mystic structures. But, in this perspective, the Haute Couture has to be distinguished from the ready-to-wear. The former determines mostly,

---

99. Karl Lagerfeld and Hubert de Givenchy still present miniskirts in their collections (*Vogue*, France, respectively August and September 1971) and Yves Saint Laurent long slit skirts (*Vogue*, September, 1971) but in these heroic structures have already been introduced "mystic" elements as marabou feathers at Karl Lagerfeld's or flowered embroideries at Yves saint Laurent's.

if not exclusively, a synthetic universe, while the latter is 50% in synthetic structures and 50% in mystic structures when the totality of the creations is being considered. Actually, the Haute Couture plays on the dialectics and the harmonization of the contraries, calls in history, and utilizes fabrics and forms that fit modern life —consequently, they mean progress, set in a context of sensuousness and sexuality. The Haute Couture especially stresses the masculine/feminine and Western/Eastern oppositions, tries to find a mediator that can be history, to annihilate or, at least, monitor these oppositions. The opposition/synthesis of the sexes, the civilizations, the historical periods, most of Yves Saint Laurent's collections over these years are a very good illustration of. On the contrary, the ready-to-wear, possibly because it borrows from a fashion that originates in the street, particularly from the Puces in Paris or from Portobello Market in London, oscillates between synthetic structures and mystic structures. As the Haute Couture, it encourages the synthesis of the sexes, thanks to the trousers that are now worn by all the women, and, to a lesser degree, the synthesis of the cultures. But it creates too long pleated skirts and dresses, with a duplication of frills, in chiffon or other light fabrics, and in general cocoon-like clothes, colors, floral prints, smooth and comfortable fabrics (linen or cotton, for instance), all being good symbols of a desire for union and intimacy, significant of the mystic structures. This mystical trend, of which Sonia Rykiel's wool provides a perfect example as far as intimacy is concerned, is at its height in 1977 with Kenzo and some other designers. It is interesting to remark that even Yves Saint Laurent, whose ready-to-wear is generally a continuation of his "synthetic" Haute Couture models with some of his well-known outfits such as the jumpsuit or the tuxedo, is also going in this mystical trend that same year with his "Rive Gauche" collection…

The importance of synthetic and mystic structures in the Seventies bears no contradiction to fashion photography. Fashion photography does accompany and reinforce it. Firstly, an important modification in the physical type of the models is to be noticed. The Sixties models' solar type, who matched with the heroic outerwear, is replaced by a whole range of girls who can represent, on the one hand, androgyny and sensuousness or, on the other hand, the eternal femininity and intimacy. In the second half of the decade, the introduction of African models on the catwalk brings an even more important nocturnal tonality.[100] But a total change in the photographic inspiration is to be seen. The Sixties' grand outdoors, generally urban outdoors with vertical lines, are replaced by a far more intimate scenery, which matches with the mystic structures of clothes. The indoor photographs or the (French, British, or even tropical) garden photographs are definitely dominant, and water

---

100. It should be noticed that a black male model and a white female model have first embodied, as a mix of the sexes and the races in a Yves Saint Laurent Rive Gauche advertisement (*Vogue,* August 1975), the confrontation-union of Africa and Europe.

is very often linked to women to signify the *Magna Mater*. But there is no better illustration of the mystic structures' importance than an advertisement for Courrège Prototype. The photograph shows a futuristic scenery, familiar to the designer, but the tubes that are part of this scenery look like intestines, a good symbol of the inversion[101] just as the clothes are, a large shirt in yellow cotton on a large skirt.

The synthetic elements of the Seventies fashion images are the very basis from which the heroic universe that is dominant between 1981 and 1987 is rebuilt. Indeed, after a short transition period, between 1978 and 1981, where 70% of the fashion images are in synthetic structures against 30% in mystic structures and heroic structures, from the early Eighties on, a return to the diurnal order in 70% of the cases can be witnessed. In this transition, Milanese ready-to-wear plays an important part. Built on the dialectics of the sexes (the Armani pantsuit) and the synthesis of historical periods (the Antiquity or Renaissance inspiration in Versace's clothes), sensuousness (destructed patterns and light fabrics), it slowly turns towards an imaginary in which ascension, light, and separation symbols are a counterpart of animal and night symbolism. Gianni Versace, who, along with Giorgio Armani, already proposed in 1978 the image of an aggressive and dangerous femininity with draped, belted, and décolleté leather sheaths, is a very good example of it. And with Versace, the whole fashion

---

101. See G. Durand, *Les structures anthropologiques de l'imaginaire*, p. 228-229.

imaginary slowly drifts away from the synthetic structures, still alive in 1981 and 1982 in Jean Louis Scherrer's and Yves Saint Laurent's Haute Couture Indian collections, to reach the heroic structures around which the images and symbols are now organized.

But the atmosphere of the images is now far more important than the forms, the colors, and the fabrics; accordingly, it becomes more difficult to tell the difference between the images of clothes and the images of fashion. One can only distinguish two different series of images. The first one makes sense in a translation from a person to clothes. Because such outwear was the outwear of a real or fictive femme fatale in the past, it embodies this kind of femininity and, consequently, stands for itself or for the models wearing it, so that, as a setting, an indoor background would suffice. The second one is where a particular piece of clothing has a relation with external elements: an outfit for which form and fabrics imply a heroic script as an advertising extension and is to be accompanied by an outdoor background with heroic elements. These two series are characteristic of the Eighties.

Designers have followed Gianni Versace, who, after meditating over female sculptures in classical antiquity, gave his very geometrical and color-contrasted dresses a touch of extreme femininity. References to the Hollywood vamp and stars of the Thirties and Forties are very frequent, as well as references to the movie thriller heroines of the same decades. Consequently, the former's black sheath dresses, panther or leopard arrays, and the latter's "pied de poule" or Prince of Wales skirt suits, trench coats, and raincoats provide models from which a whole range of clothes originates. Good illustrations are provided by some outerwear presented on Jerry Hall, who, after modeling for the front cover of a Roxy Music LP in a black skirt suit (with a very tight-fitting skirt), a fishnet veil, and a panther on a leash, was condemned to embody dangerous femininity: a panther-printed chiffon dress by Hanae Mori,[102] a Prince of Wales skirt suit with a long jacket and a tight-fitting skirt by Yves Saint Laurent, photographed by George Hurrell[103]; or a satin evening skirt suit by Yves Saint Laurent Rive Gauche[104]; and, of course, diverse sheath dresses by Thierry Mugler, for whom she is the favorite model. However, some other clothes also show a Hollywood inspiration, such as Givenchy's long panther- or zebra-printed sheaths.[105A] Dior black silk sheath dress by Marc Bohan.[106], or a Thierry Mugler Evita Perón-like skirt suit photographed in a room at the Hotel Oloffson in Port-au-Prince, Haiti.[107]

The second series of images is plain to identify. It even deploys, with a particular strength as a

---

102. *Vogue*, France, March, 1981.

103. *Ibid.*

104. *Vogue*, France, August, 1983.

105. *Vogue*, France, March, 1981.

106. *Ibid.*

107. *Vogue*, February, 1985.

compensation for the dark and deathly feminine figures, symbols of ascension. The clothes in themselves can be significant of a heroic universe, as warrior-inspired clothes by Armani and Versace, or Hell's Angels' jackets by Thierry Mugler in the 1980s, 1982, and 1984 falls, but when they are not, they find in the fashion photography images their heroic metaphor. To sumptuous clothes (Tan Giudicelli and Mugler) and close-fitting clothes (Alaia and Claude Montana) that are to be regarded as examples of pragmatic deficit, urban, mountain, or desert images are consistently linked, with vertical lines, extreme luminosity, and violent contrasts. These images provide contexts for various designers' creations (from Lagerfeld to Alaia and Ungaro and even Yves Saint Laurent), but Thierry Mugler, who is definitely the designer of this decade, is even more illustrative. Indeed, from 1979 on, he multiplies the images of skyscrapers, blue sky, the American West wilderness with mountains and deserts; of metallic structures, of geometrical and glass forms, deploying ascension symbols (parachutes on blue sky, statues of gods and heroes, etc.), images that appear as an antithesis to the devouring monster of his 1991 advertising campaign. To such a point that this universe of heroic structures has become his very definition.

The heroic universe of the Eighties fashion had its heyday in July 1987 with the Christian Lacroix Haute Couture collection. This collection was a shock to everyone. With the majesty of its forms and the luxury of the fabrics, it was more sumptuous than any collection ever seen, and, with its Mediterranean references, it was a quest for light and sun. There is little doubt that we can find an extension of this heroic universe with the stardom reached by the models at that time, the era of supermodels such as Claudia Schiffer, Naomi Campbell, Linda Evangelista, Cindy Crawford, and Christie Turlington who began their careers then. However, Christian Lacroix's collection appears as the last collection belonging to the heroic universe. And, as always, some elements do anticipate the new universe of the Nineties. Indeed, Christian Lacroix, in this 1987 collection, already introduces some synthetic elements (clothes from the nineteenth century mixed with Thirties satin fabrics, for instance), and already drifts towards mystic structures with duplication, boxing, and superposition (a satin apron with a big knot in the back on a satin dress).

Even if Haute Couture, free from ready-to-wear and prone to all experiments, tends to create majestic outfits, and even if some fashion editors ask for heroic fashion to be back,[108] most of the fashion images from the beginning of the Nineties are to be interpreted as being nestled in the nocturnal order. Actually, 80% of them or more are in synthetic or mystic structures.[109] The main characteristics of today's fashion (from the beginning of the Nineties till now) are, indeed, the confusion of historical periods, cultures,

---

108. See J.J. Buck in «Le point de vue», *Vogue*, February 1999, p. 121.

109. Only two designers, Thierry Mugler and Claude Montana, are still creating a fashion of "heroic" inspiration.

sexes (or, at least, genders), and the juxtaposition of colors and prints. These confusions and juxtapositions are plain to see at every level of the fashion images: clothes and models (every race, or melting of races, can be seen on the catwalks) and photographs (very diverse settings are multiplied and sometimes juxtaposed). But, on this synthetic ground that has become the norm — and consequently is not so significant— grows a mystic vegetation. In this respect, Jean-Paul Gaultier is certainly a true leader. In the middle of the Eighties, even if his clothes were rather in synthetic structures, he already deployed a mystic imaginary. But in the Nineties, he is definitely set in mystic structures. He melts the civilizations, the historical periods, and the sexes together. But, at the same time, he tries to dismiss the fashion model as a star: he launches his friends on the catwalk and chooses models who have an unconventional look in regard to the criteria of female beauty; he plays with the duplication of the different layers (skirt, underskirt, tunic and dress, corset worn as outerwear on a dress, etc.); he bears great attention to detail (embroideries and printed dresses); he is very careful with the sensuousness of the fabrics. His "Tonkinoise (Tonkinese)" in 1989 is a good illustration, with the West/East, masculine/feminine melting on the one hand, and with its superposition, its prints, and the care brought to motifs on the other hand. Following Jean-Paul Gaultier, draperies, pleats; soft colors; fluid, feminine, shining fabrics; prints, embroideries, and lace have multiplied and combined to create female images that go from the traditional and aerial sylph (Lagersfeld Haute Couture, fall 1995) to a whole range of romantic figures (1996), passing through diverse images, quite difficult to characterize, sometimes even new. Examples of the last ones are numerous, but we can focus on a very significant one: a long silk satin tunic dress on a skirt with a mini tail and velvet platform sandals by Prada in 1997.[110] Moreover, the pregnancy of the mystic structures in the Nineties fashion is also to be seen in the need for comfortable clothes, an almost complete fusion with clothes, and, consequently, in the development of such fabrics as viscose, and then in the sportswear that is a dominant model in the current ready-to-wear. Besides, this very pregnancy can also be seen in the experiments on clothes, far from the pragmatic function, and sometimes even from the very first function of clothes: to be worn. These experiments are deformations and prostheses seen in Vivienne Westwood's clothes, as in Viktor and Rolf's, the latter being connotative of maternity. They are also to be seen in Hussein Chalayan's fashion that oscillates between conceptual art and a reflection on clothes, the chadors in his 1998 spring collection being a good illustration of this. This fashion does present, with the minimalist style shared by Chalayan and some of his Japanese colleagues, an inner quest and a claim for mystic liaison.[111]

---

110. *Vogue*, France, February 1997.

111. That Hussein Chalayan gave "The Bed" as a title to his February 1999 New York show, in which everything was warmth, softness and comfort and the models were walking around a

"Fashion trends are the expression of what is going on inside a society" used to say Li Edelkoort,[112] the head of Trend Union, and there is little doubt that the main fashion trends that I have identified and analyzed so far with methods borrowed from Gilbert Durand provide information regarding what is going on inside the societies, and what determines the transformation and evolution of these societies.

Firstly, the orders and structures that identify a given period can be interpreted as a philosophical position. The diurnal order and the heroic structures are significant in a society governed by the power of reason, while the nocturnal order and the mystic or synthetic structures are significant in societies with other ways of reaching knowledge: sensitivity, intuition, and imagination.

G. Durand says that extreme and, to an extent, "morbid" rationalism is expressed very strongly by the heroic structures of the diurnal order[113]. Indeed, the Sixties with their dominant heroic structures are an avatar of the Prometheism that has been dominant since the eighteenth century and during the nineteenth century, of this progressive ideology that wants to plan

---

virtual hearth wearing soft brown fabrics is the best confirmation, if need be, of his mystic inspiration.

112. Quoted in *Vogue*, France, March 1995, p. 192.

113. G. Durand, *Les structures anthropologiques de l'imaginaire*, p. 209.

individual and social happiness by the way of reason.[114] Quite logically, the Eighties that belong to the diurnal order should be identically construed. But, if the heroic structures are very important, they coexist with visions of time and death, and, consequently, the Eighties imaginary shows some differences that may indicate a social positivism rather than a philosophical position.

The Seventies, when we consider the vast majority of images organized around mystic and synthetic structures, appear to question Prometheism. Compromise is the very identifier of the nocturnal order[115], and this compromise is significant of a philosophical attitude that is based on the sentiment of nature or the cosmic liaison, and oscillates between naturalism and mysticism, or, as it tries to conciliate everything, tends to syncretism. This attitude is also the attitude of the Nineties and Two thousand. But, then, the vision is mainly a naturalistic vision.

But, even more than a philosophical position, the fashion imaginary is the expression of a moral attitude towards the world and life in general, the ways a society regards itself. Once again, the four periods can be considered two by two.

The heroic universe of the Sixties is the universe of a society that is self-confident, and confident in its ability to resolve the problems that will be met and that is a conquering society; nothing seems impossible for it.

---

114. See M. Maffesoli, *L'Ombre de Dionysos. Contribution à une sociologie de l'orgie*, Paris: Méridiens, 1982, p. 156.

115. G. Durand, *Les structures anthropologiques de l'imaginaire*, p. 307.

But, at the same time, this universe, which even refuses the possibility of any other universe, has to be converted one day or the other to reach some equilibrium. And, from this perspective, the Seventies' synthetic and mystic fashion universe appears as extending and challenging the Sixties' heroic universe. The Seventies do not question the self-confidence of the previous decade, but they are reconsidering the means. They trust no more technology and progress and, back to something more concrete, they try to balance them in managing everyday life carefully and find a way of evolution in every aspect of social life. The mystic structures are significant, indeed, of a return to intimacy, of a peaceful relation with the immediate environment, and an inner well-being. The will to possess nature is replaced by the will to protect it, and escaping the world is replaced by getting inside it. As to the synthetic structures that become dominant at the end of the decade, they signify the will to harmonization between the outside and the inside, the past and the future, and the desire to conciliate sexual drives with the forces of history, to live fully every moment and to be close to the cyclic time of primitive societies.

The diurnal order of the Eighties is different from the Sixties', as I have already underlined. While the latter goes beyond the feminine theme, the former almost exclusively focuses on it and opposes strongly to visions of time and death, and its heroic structures; consequently, it is unsurprisingly dominated by female figures. If it still expresses the dynamics of self-confident societies, heading, shaped by technological progress, into the future, it mainly emphasizes a very important change in the role of the sexes that has prevailed so far. In multiplying the images of a deadly and ominous femininity, it underlines the traditional link between woman and death but, in opposing and juxtaposing these images to a heroic universe, it also manifests the social assumption of women. To a woman who appears as a threat to the power of men and to men's being and identity, is superposed a conquering woman who would bring change to societies, a woman who means progress and future. The nocturnal order and the mystic structures in which, at the end of the Eighties, the fashion imaginary enters are not an extension but a break and a change of perspective. To existential and social anguish, the answer was going into action and risk, or even in transcendence; and now, to this anguish, the answer is going back into oneself and into the limitations of morality. In other words, after the open sea wind, return to the authenticity of the village. Even if they do not have these tools of analysis, some fashion commentators are keen on this change in perspective and consider the picture offered by fashion images in the Nineties and Two thousands as the picture of a constrained society, afraid of living and being itself. "Epoque rétrécie par la morale, l'absence de risques, d'audace, la peur de s'inventer elle-même (A time shrunk by morals, the absence of risks and audacity, afraid of inventing itself)"[116]; "Esthétique du banal, esthétique du désespoir (aesthetics of banality and despair)"[117]; "Fuite hors lumière, côté calfeutré (Flight outside light, caulked life)."[118] These are some comments, the last one being a good definition, actually, of the mystic structures. These structures express indisputably a return on one's self, in intimacy, but also a distrust of desire and beauty, and no longer the desire to seduce that goes with them, as a terrible difficulty of being."

To exemplify the main anthropological structures of the imaginary, G. Durand has called in psychiatry and its definitions of mental illnesses: schizophrenia, paranoia, and autism for the heroic structures (once called schizomorphic structures); epilepsy for the mystic structures, and manic-depression for the synthetic structures. One could be tempted to extend these psychiatric classifications, valid for individuals, to societies, even if G. Durand has refused the extension and warned against the temptation. "The heroic (schizomorphic) structures are not schizophrenia; they remain and subsist in the so-called normal representations."[119]

The idea of mental health for a society, even more than for an individual, is undoubtedly highly problematic. One should not consider societies as

116. *Vogue*, France February 1993.

117. *Vogue*, France, March 1996.

118. *Vogue*, France, August 1998.

119. G. Durand, *Les structures anthropologiques de l'imaginaire*, p. 215.

schizophrenic, epileptic, or manic-depressive. However, one can consider that, on the one hand, such an order or such a structure can provide good information on the aspirations or fears of a particular societal body at a given moment in history, or on the state of society, and that, on the other hand, too large a part played by a structure claims for its conversion into another one, almost independently of historical factors,[120] that consequently, the fashion imaginary is a mold for history. In compensation, it may seem quite correct to consider that a fashion designer exclusively rooted in a particular structure shows at least a certain tendency toward some pathology. For instance, Paco Rabanne's and Thierry Mugler's creations, as the photographs inspired by them, are so deeply rooted in the heroic structures that they suggest that both designers have a mental structure close to paranoia and schizophrenia. Going in that direction may not prove necessary or even interesting, but it raises an important question. Since the fashion images provided by an entire profession (designers, models, photographers, fashion magazines, etc.) and not only by an individual have been considered, the analysis of the creation of an individual compared to the creation of a period was not a priority. But now we can focus on the relations between the imaginaries of a designer and a period with some good chance of success.

---

120. *Ibid.*, p. 141.

III

THREE DESIGNERS

CHAPTER 6

YVES SAINT LAURENT AND THE SEVENTIES

The methods utilized to identify the different trends of forty years of fashion images can be used again to describe a designer's own career. The general perspective and the methodological principles that I have developed in chapter 5, the necessity to take into account societal evolution, to cross the identifying elements of the clothing imaginary, and to consider, beyond the clothes themselves, fashion images (that is, models and photographs) are still valid. But to have them adapted to the new object, I have to stress some points.

Firstly, I have to stress the fact, and it is fairly logical, that fashion images in magazines cannot be the only object to focus on, and not even a privileged one. The main function of a fashion magazine was to play an intermediary role between potential clients and designers' creations. Through the selection made among hundreds of models by different designers, the magazine achieves a quintessence that defines the trends and displays the imagery of a particular period, a year, or a season. However, it proves impossible to reduce a designer's imagery to the small part of his or her creation that constitutes the common point of the whole fashion creation of one year. Consequently, we have to consider all of his or her collections or, at least, the most important pieces in a collection, for instance, the ones that have been promoted by the photographs.

Secondly, we have to consider that designers may change their style to fit in the main trends of a period, and accordingly, it would become impossible to speak of a personal imaginary. But we may object that this change is a free decision in their career as fashion designers and, as we will see, cannot be carried on if it is too large a step from the designer's previous options.

When we keep in mind these different points, we can consider Yves Saint Laurent's whole career, which coincides with the forty years of fashion creation we have considered and has had an important impact on the second half of twentieth-century fashion.

Fashion images created by Yves Saint Laurent from the very beginning, when he was Christian Dior's assistant, to the last collections, indisputably describe the two diurnal and nocturnal orders of the image and the three structures of these orders: heroic, mystic, and synthetic. Indeed, if we consider each collection and apply to it the 70% principle, each structure appears dominant in a particular period of time. However, over his forty years of creation, synthetic structures are dominant, and there is little doubt that they define Yves Saint Laurent's style.

In the 1966, 1967, and 1968 collections, the percentage sometimes reaches 100%. The geometric dresses (the "Trapeze" dresses and the "Mondrian" collection dresses), the antithesis of the first see-through blouses in 1966 and the nude look in 1968, the white and black colors, the stripes and the squares, materials such as leather with the black leather jacket as early as 1960 or the wooden dresses in the African collection in 1967, clothes symbolizing adventure with the sailor style in 1966 or the safari jacket in 1968, or even warrior-like with the Bambara collection in 1967, all relate to a heroic universe. The very title of some collections, at least indirectly, is illustrative: the "white" collection, the "Mondrian" collection, the "Bambara" collection, and even a kind of manifesto.

But, inside this heroic universe, is looming a synthetic universe that will be the very definition of Yves Saint Laurent's style. The first tuxedo and the "dandy-look," which respectively play on the masculine and feminine opposition and harmonization, were created in 1966 and 1967, and the first jumpsuit in 1968. This style was generalized in 1969 with the "he" style and dominated hereafter to constitute, until the end of Yves Saint Laurent's career, the referential style, even when, for a short period of time, it could be hidden by another one, heroic or mystic. From 1969 to 1977, the Haute Couture and the ready-to-wear collections were widely based —in at least 70% of the cases— on the dialectics of the sexes: the "lean-look" in 1975, and the dialectics of civilizations: the "Russian Ballets" in 1976 or the "Chinese collection" in 1978, or on calling history in the "Forties" collection —all synthetic structures that determine the most important trends of the period: androgyny, exoticism, retro. In 1977, while remaining in the nocturnal order, some mystic structures that could already be seen marginally in Yves Saint Laurent's ready-to-wear (gypsy skirts in 1970, for instance) replaced the synthetic inspiration in 1977 with the colorful and ample outfits of the Spanish and Romantic Haute Couture collections and, until 1981, coexisted within the Haute Couture and ready-to-wear collections. In the first half of the Eighties, Yves Saint Laurent promoted, with some other designers, the image of a conquering and fatale female, who was already present in the "Russian Ballets" and the "Opium" collections, creating some geometrical clothes as in the Matisse collection in 1981, while the photographs of his creations had violent and luminous contrasts. The Marceau skirt suit in 1982 is quite illustrative of the fatale femininity, even more so when photographed by Helmut Newton in a very famous 1981 photo shoot, as well as a model titled the "Panther Mermaid." However, the diurnal order and the heroic structures, even if they are important in the collections and the photographs, as the mystic structures in the 1984 spring-summer Haute Couture collection with the "Domino ciel de Paris," do not take over the synthetic structures that are still the main inspiration of Yves Saint Laurent.

In general, the synthetic structures, inasmuch as they define forms (the masculine/feminine: tuxedo and pantsuit, for instance) of what has become Yves Saint Laurent's hallmark, or an everlasting exotic inspiration, are at least 30% present in every collection in the 1978-1984 period and, consequently, quite prominent. And, at the end of the Eighties, they are dominant again. Between 1987 and 1989, the mystic structures and the heroic structures are still present (the sunflowers in the Van Gogh collection being a good example of the former, the "paradise birds" in the 1987 collections a good example of the latter), but from 1990 onwards, the synthetic ones are dominant. The dialectics masculine/feminine is now integrated into contemporary fashion and, consequently, is not as significant in synthetic structures, as well as the West/East and the time oppositions, but the opposition and harmonization of colors and fabrics in which Yves Saint Laurent is definitely the ultimate master, as the purified style that he has reached, or the very titles of his collections and the photographs, are many elements that define a synthetic universe.

Yves Saint Laurent's career is closely linked to the general trends of the Sixties, Seventies and Eighties fashion. Obviously, some designers are good examples of the trends of the Sixties such as Pierre Cardin, André Courrèges or Paco Rabanne or the trends of the Eighties such as Thierry Mugler and possibly Gianni Versace, but Yves Saint Laurent is definitely *the* designer of the Seventies. This is no revelation. Assuredly. We only have to consider the very important space occupied in the Seventies magazines or in the media by Yves Saint Laurent, or, in a materialistic perspective, the success of Yves Saint Laurent's company and the commercial empire that has been created. But the perspective that I have adopted, the imaginary one, makes clear why Yves Saint Laurent and the Seventies met, and, accordingly, what has determined his commercial success.

The meeting of personal imaginary and social imaginary raises the following questions: how has this meeting been done? What makes Yves Saint Laurent an icon of a period but also determines the forms of this period? In other words, how does he look at the world, how does he interpret it, and what are the forces driving him?

Firstly, since he has often stated that his best weapon is how he looks at his time, we can consider that he has a true intelligence of society. He is not a foreseer, and no more is he a sociologist, but he was able to see, when he was at Dior's, the limits of the postwar bourgeoisie in which he had been raised, and he was aware that a world was over and another one was beginning, with a lot of possibilities, a lot of dangers, and a lot of seductions.[121] And he feels the Seventies, the desires, and the main aspirations of this decade. As Susan Train puts it, speaking of the Russian Ballets collection: "We were in pants. And suddenly we were again dressed in long skirts and boots. He knew

---

121. L. Benaïm, *op.cit.*, p. 92-93.

the temperature of the time. He seems to know what we want before we were even conscious of it; he puts everything in order."[122] This social anticipation, Yves Saint Laurent himself has denied it, stressing the interaction between the designer and the social constraints: "dresses will change according to the events and inspirations that guide them", but it can explain the meeting of Saint Laurent with the Seventies. Nevertheless, it is not a sufficient explanation for the synthetic structures: the harmonization of the masculine and feminine, the dialectics of the cultures, and the historic rhythms that Yves Saint Laurent has imposed on a decade identified by them. They originate, to a large extent, in Yves Saint Laurent's personal history. That is where his own style finds its very origins.

The androgynous style, in the first place, appears as the expression of a particular sexual desire. Until very recent times, the masculinization of women, in art or literature, was a means to reveal and hide homosexuality that could not be expressed more directly because of all the social pressures pounding on it. From Joris-Karl Huysmans to Jean Lorrain, passing through other writers, the decadent literature at the end of the nineteenth century can provide a whole range of examples[123] Yves Saint Laurent, who was fascinated by this period, may have meditated upon. Anyway, for a man born in 1936 who used to recall that "to be a

---

122. Quoted by L. Benaïm, p. 316-317.

123. See F. Monneyron, *L'Androgyne décadent. Mythe, figure, fantasmes*, Grenoble: ELLUG, 1996.

homosexual in Oran was as [if] being a murderer," shy and introverted, the masculinization of women does appear as the only possible expression of homosexual desire. But his genius and, at least, his originality was to transfer it into an artistic form, couture, of which the human body is the main support and, consequently, that implies desire, so that, as Maurice Sachs in *Au temps du Boeuf sur le toit* already noticed about Chanel and the Twenties fashion, nothing was better to encourage homosexuality than this boy-like attitude that the women had.

Although in Saint Laurent's couture, the androgynous style, far from suppressing the woman's body, reveals femininity better than any other outfit, it remains a desire of the same. In the Sixties, when he began to be interested in the androgynous style with the sailor style and the first tuxedo in 1966, and the pantsuit in 1967, he had in mind some great heroes in dressing women: Brummell's vests, Dorian Gray's curly golden hair, scarves, makeup, Watteau's *Gilles*, and the Extravagants' high heels and jewels.[124] Later on, the androgyne becomes a real ideal, for him who is attracted by ambiguity, as for Helmut Newton, who says: "The woman dressed in a tux becomes an androgynous figure. She is not a woman but can be a very beautiful boy or a very beautiful woman."[125] But the androgyne will keep its primary function. Even if the male body can be seen more easily, as in Jeanloup Sieff's famous

---

124. L. Benaïm, p. 186.

125 . Quoted by L. Benaïm, p. 283.

photograph, when the designer poses, naked, for his first perfume campaign "Rive gauche", he is still looking for the man through his models and friends who embody the androgynous ideal, Loulou de la Falaise or Betty Catroux. He finds with Loulou the dandy and with Betty a tomboy.

The exotic inspiration that is a hallmark of Yves Saint Laurent's fashion in the Seventies also finds its motivations in his personal history, namely in his North African origins. Born and raised in North Africa, Yves Saint Laurent was destined to be a mediator between the two shores of the Mediterranean Sea. If he came to Paris at seventeen, was rapidly successful, and became the most Parisian of all the Parisian designers, he would never forget the colors and the odors of Oran, his birthplace. From 1967 onwards, every year, he would spend some months on the African continent, in Marrakesh where, with Pierre Bergé, he bought and rebuilt three houses, the latest one being the "Villa Oasis" in the Majorelle gardens. This African inspiration is obvious in his clothes, and North Africa, or, to a certain extent, Africa, is the initial pattern of his exotic inspiration. With the safari jacket, the African outerwear of the European colonist, the Bambara dresses that are European in form and African in fabrics, or, later on, the projection onto Western models of the colors and fabrics seen in the Moroccan streets, he tries to reconcile different cultures or, at least, attitudes and ways of being. Even if he extends this will of reconciliation to other civilizations such as

India or China, we always find in his clothes, regardless of the model wearing them being European, African, or Asian, a mix of French classical taste and Mediterranean sensuousness, and images of women that are not entirely Eastern but not entirely Western either.

The historical relationship initiated by Yves Saint Laurent with the "Forties" collection also has some biographical background. The "retro" style was a change after the futuristic experiments of the Sixties and an attempt to find an equilibrium with the values of the past. And, as far as Yves Saint Laurent is concerned, after a long and prolonged youth that was dedicated to the conquest of the present, the retro style appears as a return to himself. This style was a bridge between the immediate post-war period and the new Seventies decade, but for Yves Saint Laurent, it is also a bridge to his childhood in Oran. Indeed, with the return to the Forties fashion that was obliterated by Dior's "New Look,"[126] images of his childhood are privileged, and, in particular, images of his mother, Lucienne Matthieu-Saint Laurent. In a 1983 *Le Monde* interview by Yvonne Baby, Yves Saint Laurent talks about his mother in a black dress with square sleeves in a ballroom, before he was taken away from her and enrolled in a Catholic school, so that he became someone else. Actually, Lucienne in this black dress is his first fashion vision. And, thirty years later, he creates the "retro" model,

---

126. See C. Dior, *Dior et moi*, Paris: Bibliothèque Amiot et Dumont, 1956.

which was linked to his last moments of happiness in Oran.[127]

In the Seventies, Yves Saint Laurent's fashion can be regarded as proceeding from personal stable elements: the androgynous style from his homosexuality, the exotic inspiration from his North African origins, and the "retro" style from his childhood. On the contrary, specific circumstances in his life, which, at the end of the decade and at the beginning of the next decade, give new directions to his work and imagination, coincide with new trends in fashion.

Indeed, the mystic structures, as well as the heroic structures that are now characteristics of his fashion imaginary, must be related to the depression into which Yves Saint Laurent sinks. The heroic structures are not schizophrenia, and the mystic structures are not epilepsy, but they do betray in Yves Saint Laurent some tendencies, as G. Durand has pointed out in *Les structures anthropologiques de l'imaginaire*[128]. In 1977, Yves Saint Laurent, who reached stardom, but obviously lost his former enthusiasm, was ill. To the magazine *Le Point*, in December 1976, he says: "I am ill, very ill. I was already ill before the Haute Couture collection in July, but nobody noticed. But I was really depressed."[129] Alcoholic (he drinks several bottles of whisky a day)and cocaine-addicted, he is

---

127. L. Benaïm, *op. cit.*, p. 16.

128. G. Durand, *Les structures anthropologiques de l'imaginaire*, p. 310.

129. Quoted by L. Benaïm, p. 317.

regularly hospitalized at the American Hospital in Neuilly. He stumbles to the ground and is very close to epilepsy.[130] Pierre Bergé who leaves him, then, will say some years later: "Alcohol, then cocaine, then narcoleptic, Yves has never really come back to life. Instead of dying, he has continued. Yves is close to the drunkard, the aristocracy, the pop stars, the betrayed woman. He likes physical abandon. He likes being a bum. He has always said that he would end up as an old lady sitting on a box of wine."[131] Even if depression rapidly becomes the very image of Yves Saint Laurent, he keeps on creating with the utmost energy. But we can regard this depression as the very source of grand collections that put forth a mystic universe, from the Spanish and the Romantic collections to the sunflowers in homage to Van Gogh a decade later. The need for protection and something liquid that is characteristic of the mystic structures, the aquatic universe in which Yves Saint Laurent likes to rest at the time, are good witnesses: the room with mirrors in his rue de Babylone apartment in Paris, the pond of his villa in Marrakech, the lake in Deauville. There is also a reconsideration of the images of women. The androgynous figure does not disappear, but there are now women who are more women: ethereal, asexual, unreachable, as substitutes for Yves Saint Laurent's mother. In this reconsideration, the black models are, actually, very important. On their dark skin, all the colors play. And

---

130. L. Benaïm, p. 318 and 331.

131. Quoted by L. Benaïm, p. 330.

they are images of the primitive Goddess Mother in whom it is important to fuse, and they embody this mystery that the exotic inspiration tried to express: "To me, they possess what is magical in a woman. Mystery."[132]

This mystic universe is a compensation, in the imaginary, for Yves Saint Laurent's mental depression in life. And, to an extent, Yves Saint Laurent even experiences a true mystical temptation. But in the early Eighties, this temptation is replaced by an imaginary that is rooted in the diurnal order, and this is, obviously, another aspect of his depression. While the epilepsy is behind him, Yves Saint Laurent seeks refuge in his Deauville and Marrakech houses. But this autistic seclusion and this escape into schizophrenia are determining images of time and death to which are opposed images structured by heroic structures. In particular, we have the image of the femme fatale. And even if, to an extent, Yves Saint Laurent may have borrowed from the *Zeitgeist*, we may consider that this image, which he found in the symbolist and decadent literature of the late nineteenth century and that was sketched for a long time, is fostered by his mental depression. In compensation for this threatening figure of the femme fatale, images of geometrical clothing, with antithesis or abstraction that already were characteristics of his Sixties creations (the desire of a young man to reach glory and fame), are now a

---

132. *Ibid.*, p. 421.

desperate attempt not to sink into mental illness to confront and master time and death.

Permanent elements and particular circumstances in Yves Saint Laurent's personal history do explain the coincidence between Yves Saint Laurent's imagination and the fashion imagery of the different decades. But the return, from 1988 onwards, of the synthetic structures in Yves Saint Laurent's work and, above all, their indisputable prevalence over his forty years of creation pose other questions.

This pregnancy of the synthetic structures in a designer who is the best illustration of elegance is an invitation to switch over from the social study to other questions. Is not this pregnancy a means to understand why Yves Saint Laurent is the best illustration of modern elegance? In other words: are not the synthetic structures the best possible definition of Laurentian elegance? Moreover, are these synthetic structures the very definition and the very essence of elegance?

I shall try to answer these questions. But, to do so, I need to give some definitions and to make it clear what the difference is between distinction and elegance.

The different ways of dressing have been replaced with uniformity in male bourgeois attire. But in this uniformity, there are some subtle differences. With these differences was born the distinction, this new value in the history of clothes. Since the clothing revolution of the nineteenth century, to look distinguished means to remain in the framework of bourgeois apparel and to respect the codes of sobriety and uniformity, but to always go further in refinement as far as the less visible is concerned: fabrics and cut, for instance, or the concern for a particular piece of clothing such as a tie or accessories like a hat, gloves, or a cane. In short, that means to show one's wealth, as Veblen said, but also one's culture, without conspicuousness, in the details. Brummell was a good example of it since he used to say that to be well-dressed you should not be noticed.

Distinction cannot be understood but inside a specific clothing system (here the Western system). Elegance, on the contrary, can be understood outside this system. From a Western point of view, we do not say that a man from another civilization in his traditional clothes (an Arab prince or an Indian Maharajah, for instance) is distinguished-looking, but we can very well say that he is elegant when he is. On the contrary, we can underline the distinction of a man from our own civilization, but we will only find him elegant if he takes some liberty with the usual framework of Western clothes and the means of distinction. "Elegance is in the unkempt," used to say the French poet Jean Cocteau. We should not take this statement as absolute, but we should understand "unkempt" as a liberty taken from the norms of Western clothes, but also as a liberty taken from these norms at a certain moment in time, considering sex, age, or the circumstances, or as a liberty taken between a particular piece of clothing and the way it is worn. We can understand, accordingly, that the synthetic structures can define elegance, and that Yves Saint Laurent, in whom they are dominant, is the very illustration of this. We know they are a reunion of scattered elements, opposition, dialectics of contraries, but also harmonization of what is diverse, and that, in Yves Saint Laurent's creations, good examples of them can be found in androgyny, exoticism, and history.

We could object, indeed, that far from being permanent, some of the said oppositions may be totally out of date in different periods of time, or at least not as significant as they were before. The masculine/feminine opposition is a good example. Nevertheless, if, for thirty years or so, the masculine and feminine wardrobes have gotten closer, all the outfits of the former being incorporated into the latter, as far as clothes are concerned, the collective memory is still dominated by an open system for women versus a closed system for men. And since, consequently, the androgynous style can be interpreted as a step aside from clothing norms particular to each sex, if not as a protest against them, it will also mean elegance.

That is, for sure, what Yves Saint Laurent foresaw. Already in 1958, when he was designing at Dior, he did not conceive elegance as proceeding from a beautiful array but defined it as a way of living or, some years later, fascinated by the beatnik style, as a way of being oneself,[133] showing that it is always a step aside from a norm. But his fascination for the androgynous ideal that has remained present over the years and has

---

133. L. Benaïm, p. 165.

overcome initial homosexual motivations is a better example. He understands perfectly well that a multi-secular clothing system has had a strong impact on the way the sexes are regarded, but he implicitly identifies androgyny as perfection and unity. So he says: "I have chosen this suit that is a man's suit as a representation of the woman in the future. I think that twenty years from now it will still be valid; the woman's body is evolving to a thin, androgynous figure, close to a young male body, and this ambiguity is charming and seductive."[134] And his goal is to create prototypes that will never be outdated: "As the jeans that have reached perfection. (…) The jeans don't have sex; they can be worn by every man and every woman, in every season, day and night, everywhere in the world, at every age, in all social classes."[135] Actually, Yves Saint Laurent finds here, with clothes, all the characteristics of an old mythological figure.[136] And, as the androgynous body in Hellenistic sculpture[137] and in the Neo-classical painting of the early nineteenth century[138] was beauty, similarly, in Western contemporary fashion, the androgynous outfit is elegance.

---

134. Quoted by L. Benaïm, p. 229.

135. *Ibid.*, p. 302.

136. See M. Eliade, *Mephistopheles et l'androgyne*, Paris: Gallimard, 1962 and F. Monneyron, *L'Androgyne romantique. Du mythe au mythe littéraire*, Grenoble: ELLUG, 1994.

137. M. Delcourt, *Hermaphrodite. Mythes et rites de la bisexualité dans l'Antiquité classique*, Paris: PUF, 1958.

138. See F. Monneyron, *L'Androgyne romantique.*

As much as elegance, there is also seduction that is defined by the synthetic structures in general and the androgynous symbol in particular. In the Seventies, Yves Saint Laurent warned that the word seduction has replaced the word elegance. Actually, anthropology teaches us that synthetic structures are often linked to sexuality, with seduction being a first and necessary, if not decisive, step. G. Durand has insisted on the sexual aspects of the cyclic schema in diverse ancient societies' imaginaries.[139] If we consider the world of contemporary fashion, the relation is quite visible: I have already pointed out that the feminization of clothes reinforced the masculine seduction in putting forth the efficient principle, while the masculinization of clothes reinforced the femininity of women, far from alienating it. But when the always eroticized seduction fades away, what remains is elegance, far less eroticized, and maybe what we call taste. Are not these largely synthetic operations of opposing colors and then harmonizing them, of matching an Indian tunic with a Western skirt, men's pants with a women's blouse, what we call having good taste?

These elegance and taste, which Yves Saint Laurent has reached the essence of, pose the problem of his successors.

The study of a society's global imaginary and the Yves Saint Laurent imaginary shows clearly that, after a long and almost exceptional coincidence, in the Nineties these two imaginaries got farther and farther

---

139. G. Durand, *Les structures anthropologiques de l'imaginaire*, p. 384.

away from one another. Even if they are set in the nocturnal order, the synthetic structures that identify Yves Saint Laurent's creations oppose the mystic structures that define the global imaginary. In other words, Yves Saint Laurent is outdated. And if Yves Saint Laurent is outdated, it is because fashion is no longer about elegance and seduction; on the contrary, this inadequacy has no consequence for Yves Saint Laurent's Haute Couture, which remains the experimental field for a man who, at the best of his art, is searching for absolute elegance, but it threatens the ready-to-wear that has to match the period in order to sell. For Yves Saint Laurent's successor, how can one reconcile the synthetic universe of the brand and the mystic universe of a period, a style tantamount to elegance and seduction, with a general fashion from which elegance and seduction are absent? This inability to reconcile Yves Saint Laurent's timeless elegance with the exigencies of a period was plain to see in the first runway show of Albert Elbaz, who was in charge of YSL's ready-to-wear in 1999. He tried to rejuvenate the brand and to remain faithful to the line, but he did not succeed in rejuvenating the brand and, obviously, did not have the means to respect the line, showing some weaknesses in most of the pieces, as noted by Suzy Menkes in *The International Herald Tribune*.[140]

---

140. *The International Herald Tribune*, March 9, 1999, p. 9.

CHAPTER 7

JEAN-PAUL GAULTIER AND THE NINETIES

Jean-Paul Gaultier was regarded by Yves Saint Laurent himself as being his successor. And, even if his career does not span forty years of fashion, it is nevertheless worth considering. Since he was first introduced to the fashion world in the late Seventies, Jean-Paul Gaultier has had such an important impact on fashion that he should be focused on. In particular, it is worth contrasting his own imagination with the imagination of a period.

Using the same methodological tools that were used for Yves Saint Laurent, we may consider Jean-Paul Gaultier's collections, the most important pieces as the ones he has granted particular attention to. And it is clear that most of the clothing images, as the advertising images that are an extension, largely belong to the nocturnal order of the image.

From the expertise acquired in analyzing fashion images, two different periods in the designer's imaginary can be distinguished, and the first one, roughly the Eighties, can be identified as rooted in the synthetic structures. Everything seems to justify it, and, then, the spiritual filiations seen by Yves Saint Laurent between him, from the North African colonial upper middle-class and Jean-Paul Gaultier, the Parisian "titi", could be justified as well. In the first place, there are the Jean-Paul Gaultier's collections names that relate to synthetic elements. The names of two collections for women, "Barbès" in the Fall/Winter 1984-1985, and "Une garde-robe pour deux (a wardrobe for two)" in the Spring/Summer 1985, speak of multiculturalism and of androgyny. There are also Gaultier's "revolutionary" acts, as, in the same years, the skirt for men in the collection "Et Dieu créa l'homme (And then man was created)", or, some years later, in 1991, men and women collections "Adam et Eve Rastas d'aujourd'hui (Adam and Eve, today Rastas)" being presented together, for the first time ever, on the catwalk. One may certainly object that the names could be misleading and do not describe what the collections really are, or that the acts are deceiving and do not live up to the expectations. Nevertheless, when the collections are closely considered, they do correspond to what was anticipated by their names, and as long as the fabrics, colors prints are concerned, they belong to a synthetic universe. Jean-Paul Gaultier's imaginary in the Eighties is grounded on the dialectics of the sexes, the meeting of cultures, or on the relation to time and history. The most noticeable models are playing with the first one, as a long skirt worn by a very manly model for the Fall/Winter 1985-1986… woman collection, the very well-known conical breasted dress in 1984-1985 photographed by Jean-Baptiste Mondino on a woman for the video *How to do that?*, and by Paolo Roversi on a man, or the advertisement for the "A wardrobe for two" collection showing both a woman and a man in a halterneck. The emphasis on history is also an everlasting temptation in the Eighties collections, with the first corsets in the Spring/Summer 1983 woman collection, that will be seen again all along the decade, as the "Wedding Cage Dress" in the Spring/Summer 1989 "Le Tour du monde en 168 tenues" collection. When the form itself does not call in the other sex, another place or a different time, the juxtaposition of a red jacket with black and yellow stripes and a black scarf with white dots for "La concierge est dans l'escalier" in the Spring/Summer 1988 suggests synthetic structures. The distance taken by Jean-Paul Gaultier from the clothing and fashion system may also appear as the very principle of this synthetic universe. Caricature and irony play such an important role in his creations that they can be interpreted as a form of synthesis, when is juxtaposed in the same image the existing code and its questioning. The conical breasted dress is a good example. In caricaturing femininity, it annihilates femininity.

But, this ironical distance is also, to some extent, an introduction to the mystic universe hidden by the synthetic one. Things are not all acquired once and for all. Elements that have been interpreted as belonging to the synthetic structures in the Eighties, indeed, could very well be interpreted, later on, as mystic structures.

It proves more difficult, as it was noticed above, to consider as significant of synthetic structures, outfits that, after the Sixties and Seventies revolution carried on by a designer such as Yves Saint Laurent, have been integrated ever since in the fashion world and are worn by everyone. Thus, androgyny, exoticism, or the relation to history, becoming usual fashion trends, have obviously lost their synthetic dimension. Gaultier is going very far when androgyny is concerned, going where no one even dared to go, as when "retro" is concerned in reintroducing, for instance, the corset. No doubt. But actually, his extremism deters a genuine synthesis. If we focus on the dialectics of the sexes, it is clear that, far from reaching this subtle harmony achieved by Yves Saint Laurent, most of the time Gaultier juxtaposes heterogeneous elements identified as masculine or feminine. And with this juxtaposition, rather than fusion, confusion is achieved, which is significant of the mystic structures of the imaginary.

Many Gaultier's fashion images, in the Eighties, reveal these mystic structures. They can be, indeed, clearly identified in 30% of the images. These are some very well-known photographs, as, in 1984, the photograph of a navy blue woollen dress draped around the shoulders with, in the background, a lake and mountains, the whole scenery suggesting the mystic fusion with nature.[141] Or, in 1986, the photograph of a

---

141. *Vogue*, France, August 1984.

long leather skirt and ruffled underskirt with the ocean and rocks in the background.[142] The mystic structures are also well expressed by Gaultier's taste for symbols of inversion such as superposition or duplication, or symbols of intimacy such as prints and an extreme care for details. This taste is recurrent and, actually, one of the best identifications of Gaultier's fashion. Good illustrations of it are the "Bag Ladies" in 1986, "The Tonkinese" in 1989, or a printed slip dress worn over viscose flowered trousers.[143] The mystic structures are expressed by a whole range of colors, the use of adhering materials, or this sense of abstraction and conceptualization, significant of a mystic return in oneself, to be seen in the Fall/Winter 1989-1990 collection with an exposed seam jacket.

The mystic universe that is to be found in some Eighties models is largely developed in the Nineties. As Gaultier gets older and more self-disciplined, the trend that defines his fashion becomes even more relevant. Indeed, his main creations, which multiply symbols of inversion and intimacy, are organized around mystic structures that parallel the fading of the androgynous inspiration, while exotic and historical themes are now ironically used.

When we consider Gaultier's main collections for women in the Nineties, the elements that could be interpreted as synthetic have almost totally disappeared and have been replaced by large pregnancy-like forms,

---

142. *Vogue*, February 1986.

143. *Vogue*, March 1989.

reduplication, superposition, and inversion, pleated and draped dresses; by materials that adhere to the skin, comfortable wools, motifs and prints, embroideries, and incrustation. In the "Rabbinic" collection in Fall/Winter of 1993-1994, or in the "Monghol" collection in Fall/Winter 1994-1995, no Hebraic and Monghol exoticism is to be seen but only long and large woollen coats and chapka-like hats, on the one hand, and comfortable shearling jackets, damask silk jacquard pajamas, and printed quilted parkas, on the other hand. Simultaneously, most of the collections develop a superposition of dresses and tunics, dresses and under-dresses, dresses and petticoats, the silk velvet apron-like dress with rose prints in old black lace, on grey silk tulle petticoats in the Winter 1997-1998 Haute Couture collection being a good example of.[144] And even the rather heroic cowboy style is reinterpreted by Gaultier in a mystic way, with superposition, as for this brown pleated skirt over red petticoats in the Spring/Summer 1998 ready-to-wear collection.[145]

Ample, pleated, draped outfits, incrustations, embroideries, all are recurrent in Gaultier's Nineties collections and appear as significant of the mystic structures of his imaginary. A white dress under white draperies, embroidered cardigans in the Spring/Summer 1998 ready-to-wear collection,[146] or a long black faille silk trench coat in the 1998-1999 Haute

144. *Vogue*, France, September 1997.

145. *Vogue*, France, February 1998.

146. *Ibid.*

Couture collection[147] are some significant examples among plenty of others. The utilization of outfits and accessories borrowed from the world of sport that, since they are comfortable, can be regarded as symbols of intimacy are other examples, as are the sneakers worn on the catwalk by some models in the Winter 1997-1998 ready-to-wear collection.[148] At last, there is, of course, this inversion of outwear and underwear, Jean-Paul Gaultier is the initiator of. He does not transform anymore, as he did in the Eighties, some old underwear, namely the corset, in outwear, but he uses directly bras, corset and garter belt as outwear. Some particular models in his early Nineties collections are already illustrative, as a bra visible under sequin fishnet in 1990 or, in 1992, a silk corset and garter belt under a transparent tulle train. But, we all know that this inversion was made popular by the singer Madonna he designed the stage costumes for, who appeared on stage in corset and garter belt.

It results clearly from the above that Jean-Paul Gaultier's imagination meets the late Eighties fashion imagination, but it coincides better with the Nineties fashion imagination. Even if Jean-Paul Gaultier was worshipped very soon by the artistic avant-garde, there is no doubt that this coincidence explains better than anything else his commercial and media success. As Yves Saint Laurent was *the* fashion designer of the

---

147. *Joyce*, September-October 1998.

148. *Vogue*, France, August 1997.

Seventies, Jean-Paul Gaultier is indisputably the fashion designer of the Nineties; he determines the main trends. And, if filiations are to be found between Yves Saint Laurent and Jean-Paul Gaultier, that is where they have to be found, far more than in a false likeness in the synthetic themes of androgyny, exoticism, and "retro". Actually, they both personify the couture spirit in a particular period.

But they personify it very differently. While Yves Saint Laurent personifies it in developing his imaginary from his personal life, Jean-Paul Gaultier develops his own imaginary more independently, less dramatically and with some distance. At least, personal concerns are far less visible than they were for Yves Saint Laurent's, and even if some could be found they are not so intense. We have to consider, too, that times have been changing, and that social constraints have not such an impact on sexuality as they have had decades earlier, and especially on homosexuality that need not to be indirectly expressed anymore. Consequently, Jean-Paul Gaultier could be seen as a good sociologist, who assumes his own phantasms, is involved in the general atmosphere of the period, but observes too with some distance and objectivity what is changing in the social world. His main weapon is the way he sees his time and the world, possibly even more than Yves Saint Laurent, for he is less prone to be diverted by personal elements.

Two main operations in Jean-Paul Gaultier's approach of fashion can be identified. They can be identified all along his production, but they also correspond to the two different moments of his imaginary. The first operation is an operation of survey and analysis (and of caricature) of all the fashion constituent elements, the second one an operation of translation of an atmosphere, Gaultier depicting himself as a translator of his time.

Jean-Paul Gaultier was born in 1952 and he was twenty years old at the very beginning of the Seventies, when he started working firstly at Pierre Cardin's and then at Patou's. His first steps in the fashion world are contemporary to social movements such as Women's Liberation and Gay's Liberation that have deeply impacted Western societies and, as a consequence to the questioning of the traditional relations between the sexes, the sexual roles and the masculine and feminine identities. And, as he develops his own fashion in the Eighties, he positions himself in this questioning. He is part of a protesting period, and he attacks, with his creations, the representations of masculinity and femininity, but he does caricature too the new prejudices. Then, his fashion is to be regarded as a kind of figurative sociology.

Jean-Paul Gaultier is researching all the stereotypes of femininity and masculinity put forth by clothes. His fashion, indeed, is a kind of archaeology of feminine outfits with, as fieldwork, his own childhood memories, the feelings of a boy brought up in the Parisian suburbs and discovering what femininity is all about in the magazines and with his great mother as an initiator. Accordingly, skipping over the Sixties and Seventies, he rediscovers all the erotic attire of the object-woman, lingerie and accessories, from the corsets[149] to the padded bras, passing through high stiletto shoes, and also stresses on fitting dresses or cleavage as hallmarks of femininity. Likewise, he concentrates on the main figures of the masculine wardrobe, and tries to show the different sides of masculine identity, as epitomized by the very names of his collections for man, in 1985-1986: «Joli Monsieur (Pretty Sir)», and in 1986-1987: "French Gigolo". The irony is obvious when Jean-Paul Gaultier, who considers that sexual roles are only a game, changes the perspective and projects on men, characteristics or oppositions usually devoted to women: the object-man, the fatal man, the sexy man and the child man.

But, if these different fashion figures appear as caricatures of masculinity and femininity seductive weapons and, consequently, of sexual identities, the irony attacks as well the questioning by feminist and homosexual movements of these very weapons and identities. Since, in doing so, Gaultier may have encouraged a rehabilitation of these weapons and identities, or, at least, to have revisited some traditional outfits, some journalists have lambasted Gaultier for transforming women in prostitutes for fetishism. But,

---

149. He explained it was because he discovered as a child a pink laced corset in his grand mother's closet and was fascinated then by what appeared to him as a secret that he has wished to make this piece of lingerie up to date again.

he rather plays with the male/female roles where each sex has to explore its own stereotypes.

Jean-Paul Gaultier is also caricaturing the exotic scheme. He does not question the exotic inspiration, definitely important in the Western clothing reconsideration, but he attacks the extensive utilisation made by some of his predecessors. As a provocation to the aristocratic far away travels, he comes back to popular Paris, of which Yvette Horner's accordion, Marcel Carné's movies and the Hotel du Nord are illustrative. And, when, later on, he uses his own exotic themes, he caricatures the East, the all-time favourite exotic theme of the designers. In choosing Mongolia as the main theme of his 1994-1995 Fall/Winter collection, rather than the refinements and magnificence of Persia, India or China, he refuses the usual exotic locations and also protest against a whole fashion tradition. And, when he chooses, as a photographic scenery for his fall/winter 1993-1994 "Homage to the Jewish People" collection, Brooklyn instead of Jerusalem, he westernizes the East to which he denies any exoticism.[150]

This "deconstruction" strategy made Jean-Paul Gaultier a true *Culture Hero*, but this strategy is also an introduction to the Nineties fashion. It anticipates it and provides some of its major forms. Gaultier used to say in the Eighties: "I love everything. Everything can be beautiful or ugly. I love different kinds of beauty", and in caricaturing, de-caricaturing, re-caricaturing, he

---

150. *Vogue*, France, August 1993.

already mixes everything. And, this confusion of everything will characterize the next decade fashion imaginary, paving the way to superposition, duplication, and, more generally, to the inversion and intimacy symbolism that is to define fashion.

Gaultier is, indeed, one of the best promoters and producers of this new fashion imaginary. While his own Eighties fashion appears as a figurative sociology of the main questions of the period, his Nineties fashion is rather a symbolic anthropology of the fear and anguish of a whole generation. And, he is not anymore a simple observer and caricaturist, but a translator, since he represents in clothes and fashion images what is not to be represented, namely a societal atmosphere.

All Jean-Paul Gaultier's creations, for almost twenty years, are illustrative. Many of his clothes are the translation into images of the aspirations that are to be found in the social field. This translation can be seen in what is the best identification of his creations: superposition, reduplication, and inversion, as the inversion of outwear and underwear, but also in materials and accessories that are significant of comfort or minute work. They all have to be interpreted as the expression of a return on one's self, a desire of depths and a yearning for security, intimacy and authenticity.

The translation is generally directly achieved, but it can also be indirectly carried out. To be more precise, it occurs after a first operation the street (or a subculture) has spontaneously but imperfectly achieved, expressing in clothes a vision of the world. And, the translation then aims at giving form and style to what was spontaneous and basic in the street. Indeed, some of Gaultier's clothes are reaching the very essence of the street phenomenon without betraying it. In the Fall/Winter 1992-1993 collection, the outfit displaying a spoon and other kitchen tools is a stylization of cyberpunk clothing[151] could be a good example. But this stylisation is operating on a larger scale. The Jean-Paul Gaultier's attempt has to be interpreted as an attempt to give form to what has no form, to the chaos and confusion that are the main characteristics of high street fashion. Elegance, as I have previously pointed out, is synthesis, then Jean-Paul Gaultier's fashion is elegance of the non-elegance.

This quintessence/stylization of the street that Gaultier is achieving could be illustrative of the idea that, if, in the Seventies, fashion was still imposed from above, two decades later, the street is dictating it. But, a closer survey shows, on the contrary, how important the designer is, as a designer of models. Indeed, if we parallel Gaultier's and Saint Laurent's ways, they are not as opposed as they seem to be, the former being an imitation of the street and the latter imposing its models onto the street, but they are only two different ways to create models. When Yves Saint Laurent, lost in his own world, imposes it onto the street that recognizes some of its aspirations, Jean-Paul Gaultier looks at the street to reach a quintessence that, in turn, will become

---

151. On the cyberpunks, see. T. Polhemus, *op. cit.*, p. 124.

a model for a larger body of people. The methods are different, but the results are the same. The artist-designer and the sociologist-designer are getting close in the end.

CHAPTER 8

CHRISTIAN LACROIX AGAINST THE GRAIN

Christian Lacroix, like Jean-Paul Gaultier, began his career at the end of the Seventies, first at Guy Paulin's and then at Jean Patou's. However, he really entered, in the second half of the Eighties, the small world of fashion and the even smaller world of Haute Couture, which was at that time regarded as dying and that he has contributed to keep alive. Consequently, he does not have Yves Saint Laurent's longevity, which allows for the comparison of one individual's creation to forty years of fashion creation, and he does not embody, as Jean-Paul Gaultier does, a period, even if his creations were always awaited. But what makes Christian Lacroix so interesting, and the reason I had to focus on him in this very last chapter, is that he is actually out of step with his time and never seems to coincide with the *Zeitgeist*. Indeed, as he said himself, he is against the grain.

When we look at Christian Lacroix's collections, what catches the eye is the permanence and the unity of their inspiration. It may be objected that this inspiration is not inscribed in such a long time that we can witness major changes. But, beyond these considerations, not really decisive, since Jean-Paul Gaultier, over the same duration, showed more contrasts, it is true that Christian Lacroix's fashion does not span all the possible combinations of the Western wardrobe —Christian Lacroix used to stress that we often only have one thing to say. It is mainly a women's wear fashion, in Haute Couture for sure and, except for some ties for men, in the ready-to-wear, but it is a feminine fashion too. Indeed, the designer holds on to the traditional sexual dimorphism of the Western way of dressing and clearly favors the open system. Many of his models are dresses or skirts, long or short, tight or large, pencil skirt or ruffle skirt, but dresses or skirts.

Accordingly, the mix and juxtaposition of genders do not seem to be as determinant for Christian Lacroix as they were, respectively, for Yves Saint Laurent or Jean-Paul Gaultier. And, if we keep utilizing the hermeneutic perspective adopted, the synthetic structures do not seem to be the structures organizing his imaginary. Aside from the androgynous theme, exoticism and the reference to history often are, as we have seen, the identifier of a synthetic universe. However, these two other elements, when they are not missing, cannot be interpreted anymore as such. The exotic dimension, calling for culturally and geographically distant horizons —Africa and Asia, actually— is quite rare. It is limited to Africa with, in 1988, skirts with African art-inspired motifs, but it is not a harmonization or even dialectics of the contraries, only a transposition on Western clothes of the pictograms of another culture. The historic dimension is far more visible but does not present this "coherence in the contrast"[152] of the historic structure which is "at the heart of the notion of synthesis."[153] In Christian Lacroix's creations, a synthetic effort rarely tries to relate antithetic terms. Consequently, rather than mastering time, it is at best forgetting time, but quite often it ends up in the outright annulment of time, as I already noticed above.

It is difficult, indeed, to identify in Christian Lacroix's imaginary synthetic structures, while the heroic structures and the mystic structures are far easier to see. From the beginning of his career, his imaginary has been divided into these two other structures. However, and it is assuredly his originality, far from dividing it in a succession or a simultaneity constituted by a simple equality of the occurrences, they divide it by staying mixed together. In other words, the universe of the Arles designer is *both* a heroic and a mystic universe, with a large majority (more than 70%) of the clothes and fashion images pertaining indisputably to both universes.

Some of his creations, at the time Christian Lacroix was still working at Jean Patou's, certainly frame images of a vamp or a femme fatale, such as a Bianchini-Férier lamé crushed velvet sheath dress with a cut back and waist and a funnel-shaped neck, or a velvet top dress with a square cleavage in the back and a draped,

---

152. G. Durand, *Les structures anthropologiques de l'imaginaire*, p. 406.

153. *Ibid.*, p. 410.

stitched, short skirt in gold lamé.[154] But they are still an introduction to his creations to come. Images of time that unfold a dark symbolism, they manifest this anguish of death, to which the heroic imagination opposes, and the mystic imagination euphemizes. And, indeed, as a response to a first mortiferous inspiration, both imaginations are to activate and ally one another to define Christian Lacroix's fashion at the end of the Eighties and in the Nineties. This fashion is constituted by elements that can be regarded, in fact, as significant of the heroic and mystic structures of the clothing and fashion imaginary. On the one hand, there is this taste for the stately and the ceremonial that, better expressed in Haute Couture than in ready-to-wear, is quite synonymous with pragmatic deficit, a trend towards conceptualization that often is on par with abstraction and tends to geometry, a play with bodies and clothes that is not far from antithesis, or even clothing (long ball gowns, for example), or accessories (headdresses and hats) and bright colors and heavy jewels that display an ensemble of ascensional symbols and spectacular symbols of light and sun. On the other hand, there are amplitude and duplication (ruffled or draped dress), pleated or synthetic materials adhesive to the body, sumptuous and sensuous fabrics of all colors, and minuteness of the details with lace and embroideries, patchwork,[155] and other diverse incrustations, and more

---

154. *Vogue*, France, September 1986.

155. The patchwork is one of Christian Lacroix's main contribution to the evolution of fashion, that consists to assemble on a first drawing pieces of fabrics.

generally, a hymn to the Eternal Feminine and the *Magna Mater* that carries a symbolism of intimacy.

Of this heroic-mystic universe, numerous combinations between heroic elements and mystic elements are possible, and several series can be distinguished. When we take the heroic elements as a starting point, four major series can be considered.

The first one, which often refers to history and is more visible in the Haute Couture collections, draws on the stately and the ceremonial, has no regard for the exigencies of functionality and comfort while playing with the rolling-up, the draped, the pleated, the colors, the incrustations, or being placed under the reign of gold and fairy. It is, actually, paradigmatic of Christian Lacroix's most noted creations: his Spring-Summer 1987 dresses for Jean Patou (draped empire dress in white Bucol taffeta; long strapless dress with pouf in vermilion organza opened on a lace jersey; or jean-stitched "semi-crinoline" dress in ivory silk dupion[156]); of these large chain-printed, flower-striped skirts with Seratium taffeta pouf and draped blouse with provençal scarf in Seratium flower muslin for his first fall-winter 1987 collection[157]; of this big damask and stole skirt with a halter bra in old gold brocade underlined by patinated and embroidered metal[158]; of this silk metallic dress with stone-embroidered corset for the Haute Couture spring-summer 1996 collection photographed

---

156. *Vogue*, March 1987.

157. *Vogue*, September 1987.

158. *Vogue*, September 1995.

by Marc Hispard for *Elle*, or of most of his wedding dresses, as a heart-embroidered satin corset on an iridescent tulle skirt with a removable train, photographed for US Vogue.

Another series, a variant of the former, is aligned with artistic models. Graduated in art history, Christian Lacroix, far more than other designers, tries to transpose in fashion some art forms, particularly those of Mannerism and the Baroque Era. This transposition combines geometrization and ornateness. As Valérie de Givry points out, coherence in instability, richness of contrasts, the constant swing between the neatness of the structures and the vertigo of the adornment, between rigor and romance, between Apollonian nature and Dionysian drives unveil the oppositions of Christian Lacroix's space that are close to the outstanding beauty of the Baroque facades.[159] Two outfits are indeed very illustrative: the Astrate outfit in the fall-winter 1988-1989 Haute Couture collection, in which the twists seem to have been inspired by Bernini's canopy of Saint Peter's Basilica, and a navy blue linen evening gown on a silk faille bloomer in the spring-summer 1991 Haute Couture collection. Additionally, a splendid gown from the spring/summer 1998 Haute Couture collection reminds us of Pontormo's Deposition of the Capponi Chapel in the Florence Santa Felicità Church.

A third series, more relative to the ready-to-wear that Christian Lacroix inaugurated in 1988, then

---

159. See Valérie de Givry, *Art et mode*, Paris: Editions du Regard, 1998, p. 55.

developed from 1994 with the "Bazar" collection, works on antitheses: white/black, light/shadow, veiled/unveiled, and favors the draped, the pleated, or the rolled-up, when it does not focus on the amplitude, the printing, the embroideries, or the incrustations. Some arrays in the fall-winter 1987 collection already fall into this series, as, to only give one example, a quilted and printed Ghioldi silk skirt and a Ghioldi triangle tweed jacket with basques and a draped scarf and Scottish taffeta cuffs, or the black velvet "diabolo" gown with black sleeves for the fall-winter 1988-1989 collection. But the best example is to be found in the fall-winter 1991-1992 Haute Couture collection with this long strapless dress with chiffon and black lace vest, before others, no less significant, are to be seen in the ready-to-wear collections, as a mid-calf black warp skirt and a white crepe wide-opened jacket in the spring-summer 1996 collection.

A last series is constituted by an ensemble of clothes or pieces of clothing that do appear as ascensional, spectacular, or diairetic symbols, but that are balanced by diverse prints, embroideries, incrustations, patchworks, and endless plays on colors. These are the clothes that connote fire, light, and sun, but, at the same time, show an extreme minuteness in the details, as the bullfighter's costume created by Christian Lacroix in 1991-1992 for the toreador Chamaco, and all those close to it, such as a gold-embroidered velvet jacket or a red skirt inspired by the picadors' horses' caparison. There are also these images of flame women stimulated by a red taffeta camisole with a bubbling collar and sleeves worn over a long bell skirt in the fall-winter 1991-1992 collection, a grand indigo and orange bustier with its train, and a red sheath skirt in the spring-summer 1995 collection"[160] or a velvet, satin, and Chantilly dress with a light faille coat in the spring-summer 1996 collection"[161]. At last, there is this solar image of an "Eastern Goddess" in a painted and embroidered lycra leotard photographed by Mario Testino in 1990. Or the image, solar too, of an odalisque in an organza T-shirt embroidered with roses and black lace, and a vanilla satin, tulle, and Chantilly draped skirt seen in the Haute Couture runway show of the spring-summer 1995 collection.[162]

When Christian Lacroix's fashion is studied with imaginary methods, it is clear that he is less against the grain than one might think at first and than he used to say. In particular, if he is not entirely in the Nineties like Jean-Paul Gaultier, he is sufficiently inside not to be outside.

The dual anchor of Christian Lacroix's imaginary, in the heroic structures of the diurnal order as well as in the mystic structures of the nocturnal one, makes him embody, or at least meet, the periods framed by both structures. Thus, he does appear in his first Haute Couture collection in July 1987, as already noted

---

160. *Vogue*, March 1995.

161. *Vogue*, March 1996.

162. *Vogue*, March 1995.

in a chapter above, as the apogee and the ultimate step of the heroic universe in which the beginning of Eighties fashion was set,[163] but he does fit well in the mystic universe that defines the next decade. In other words, the heroic components of his imagination have permitted his arrival in the fashion world, while the mystic components have allowed his staying in it.

If we concentrate now more precisely on the Nineties, when Christian Lacroix became a prominent designer, the coexistence of the two orders of the image is surely the best way to understand how his fashion creation has been received. On the one hand, we can consider that its success comes from the mystic structures that, in part, underpin it and underpin too the entire fashion of the decade. On the other hand, that it is not a total success —the commercial success of the ready-to-wear, after a promising start, has not been confirmed— can be related to the mystic structures only underpinning it in part and leaving for another part the heroic structures, unusually for the time, to dominate. Aside from essentially commercial considerations, that is how Christian Lacroix is regarded among his female customers, that can be explained by this coexistence of a heroic universe and a mystic universe in the designer's imaginary. The mystic universe that invaded fashion and has the significations that we know: fearful return on oneself, desire for

---

163. The *Time*'s cover devoted to Christian Lacroix in February 1988, after his second Haute Couture collection is, in this respect, a good illustration. Not only it consecrates a creator but it sumes up a time period.

depth, need of authenticity, intimacy, and safety, is today pregnant. And Christian Lacroix certainly draws on it, but while drawing on it, he adds a heroic dimension that gives it that lustre, that energy, it is not accustomed to. For that, many young or older women can, indeed, be appreciative. Particularly, those who, while partaking in the current *Zeitgeist*, retain something of the Eighties heritage, as the desire to conciliate traditional feminine values with a conquering and self-assured femininity —those, in short, who still want to shine, even for a very brief moment in the high society life. With him, women find again something of the stately, that Haute Couture was in the past more or less synonymous, but it is also some natural "heroic" trends of the Haute Couture, becoming entirely part of the contemporary mystic universe, that are trivialized. Anyhow, Christian Lacroix's fashion, well rooted in its time, has the merit of expressing, even on a minor tone, a dynamics and a conquering spirit that is a light of hope in the ambient gloom.

This duality of the imaginary, which is the originality, and, to an extent, the strength of the Arles designer, neither originates in a personal history like Yves Saint Laurent nor in the sharp survey of societies like Jean-Paul Gaultier. Unless we consider it originates in both of them. For it is determined, firstly, by Christian Lacroix's fidelity to his native region, the Camargue.

An important number of clothes designed by Christian Lacroix, at least in the collections that made him famous, are, indeed, as it was often noted, the transposition, in the late twentieth century Haute Couture, of the Provence traditional costumes and, more precisely —the distinction being not meaningless — of the Camargue ones. And, that is true that the images sparked by these costumes are ambivalent and pertain to the heroic structures as to the mystic structures. These are, as we have seen, the toreador's costume and its Camargue equivalents that share a solar and intimate symbolism, but these are also, to a lesser degree, the costumes of the girls from Arles that combine great sumptuousness with superposition, duplication and diverse printings. Moreover, in transposing them in Haute Couture, Christian Lacroix reinforces, almost automatically, this ambivalence. On the one hand, he is bound to develop the stately and then increase even more the pragmatic deficit; on the other hand, he has to care for every detail, and make every color meet. In the twentieth century, as François Baudot remarks, in all the domains of taste, past, a symbol of conservatism, has been opposed to future, synonymous of hope. Lacroix is among those who, at the beginning of the Eighties, has been breaking this too simplistic duality[164]. And, more generally, we can certainly consider that, in breaking this duality and preferring a fashion that relives the past to make it timeless, as, for example, the well-known mini-crinoline and the big-knotted apron in the fall-winter 1987-1988

---

164. F. Baudot, *Christian Lacroix*, Paris: Assouline, p. 13.

collection, Christian Lacroix juxtaposes the two orders of the image.

Beyond clothes strictly speaking, the images of woman integrate and juxtapose these two orders of the image. Far from presenting, as is usually done, on one side the mortiferous femininity of the diurnal order and on the other side the maternal, aquatic, or telluric femininity of the mystic structures, Christian Lacroix proposes far less well cut, far more complex and, in a sense, far more balanced images of woman. And, when they are not determined directly by clothes, they also originate in the Camargue and develop inside a Mediterranean culture. Thus, the maternal figure of the Virgin Mary may very well become in the designer's imaginary the Black Virgin of the gypsies in Saintes-Maries-de-la-Mer or a Sevillian Macaréna covered with layers of veils and precious jewels, when she is not this solar virgin, synonymous of ascetic purifications, who symbolizes his sense of transcendance and inspire many of his wedding dresses. Conversely this woman, somehow fatale, wearing scarlet suits, stiletto heels, panther-skin hat, huge earrings, hair cut short and heavily made-up, who recalls women in Arles in the Sixties is not in total opposition to the maternal figure and can even be transformed into the image of a distant, mysterious, and loved woman, better approximation of the Eternal Feminine[165].

No matter how they proceed, the integration and the juxtaposition of the two orders of the image

---

165. C. Lacroix, *Péle-Méle*, London: Thames and Hudson Ltd, 1996.

appear assuredly as a kind of synthesis and, consequently, as a form of elegance, if, as I have suggested in the chapter on Yves Saint Laurent, elegance that is always a gap from a norm comes from a synthesis that reduces it. Here, the synthesis does not define synthetic structures through rhythmic symbols and schemes, but is the rough meeting of heroic and mystic structures. Rather than in interiority it is to be seen in exteriority. It is a synthesis that proves difficult to exist and is only achieved with the violent crash of elements that were firstly opposed. Then, the elegance that is achieved, rather than being achieved on its own, is, as Christian Lacroix himself puts it, "an elegance that is to be noticed."[166]

Since this form of elegance derives, directly or indirectly, from a meditation on a particular region, actually a Southern European region, could it not be related to cultural characteristics and be defined as Mediterranean? Actually, it is not affiliated with a particular geographical area. Another source of inspiration for Christian Lacroix was England and the London eccentric fashion of the Sixties, Carnaby Street, and Kensington Market, which juxtaposed the most incompatible fabrics, leather and silk, velvet and jeans, the most different motifs, stripes and prints, and even clothes from different cultures. And it proves that his elegance has no particular homeland but is simply a personal trend. It is, indeed, another option, more

---

166. *Ibid.*

dramatic than Yves Saint Laurent's, of that search for elegance that is always a harmonization of contraries.

CONCLUSION

At the end of this study on clothing and fashion, the reader, and the author himself, could express some fright. In trying to get clothes out of the frivolity they have been maintained, and still are kept, haven't we drifted into another excess? In other words, in trying to grant clothes a central position in the sociological approach, don't we explain the world with a piece of fabric or, at least, don't we look at the world through a chunk of silk or shantung?

The impression that this essay could stimulate is by no means scandalous. Should not every essay exaggerate, to be adhered to, its very point of view? Nevertheless, I would like to try to dissipate the impression, to bring some nuances and mitigate what can be seen as too systematic.

We can plead that when we can't freely exercise our choice, it is far better to know rather than to ignore the determinism that is at the origin of individual behavior or collective practices. However, what seems, in the first instance, quite unacceptable is that an activity like fashion, still regarded as derisory by many, could determine so efficiently representations and, consequently, weigh so decisively on the destinies of a society in which not much room is left for the spectator-consumer's liberty, and that, in compensation, such great power is granted to the designer.

Among those different points, it proves rather easy to rebuke the third one. It suffices to keep in mind that clothing creation is a complex phenomenon and not the creation of one creator but of an ensemble of creators, or, more precisely, an ensemble of creations that are not far sometimes to become anonymous, which does reduce the power of the designers. It could be added that the power that we may be prone to grant them is no real power since they never assume it as such, and it never tends to a particular end.

Likewise, the idea that clothes and their imagery exert such a dictatorship on representation that they determine the economic basis has to be nuanced. If clothes may indeed model individual and collective behavior and if their imagery may, at least indirectly, determine economic behavior, that is not in a totalitarian way. On the one hand, this very function, whenever it may be prominent as it directly applies to the body, the clothing creation shares it with other forms of creation: literary, artistic, cinematographic. On the other hand, the clothing imagery comes from the socioeconomic context as much as it creates this context. An interaction is thus established that excludes any form of hegemony.

It is the third reluctance, the one linked to the absence of individual liberty, that finally is the most difficult to lift. Due to the complex processes of identification and imitation I have stressed, individuals can never escape the clothing models imposed upon them and, consequently, they always take part in the general atmosphere. However, if a space of liberty cannot be found *in itself*, one can notice that, inside the dominant clothing models, an ever greater number of clothes leave some room for individual choice. Actually, the very act of getting dressed appears as a mix of determinism and free will, or, to put it in more usual words, as a mix of individualism and conformism (today conforming oneself to a general atmosphere rather than a singular social code).

Since it appears from this last consideration that, even if clothes do not make the man, there is no doubt that they make society (or the societies), it dismisses at the same time another fundamental objection that this book could raise: the one concerning the possibility of reading the state of society through the clothes that this society creates and wears.

Actually, this proposition has nothing outstanding. It is well admitted that the atmosphere of a historical period can be better read thanks to literature, cinema, or, more generally, to the ensemble of its artistic creations. Why couldn't it be read through clothes? Because clothes entertain a closer relation with the body and imply a larger public, their heuristic value is even assured to be higher. Nonetheless, this reading is less easy and immediate than we may think it would be. But, if we provide ourselves with the means to carry it on, we can go far beyond banal observations and deeply penetrate below the social surface to reveal the fears and aspirations of a society. The approach that was adopted and has allowed reaching through the clothing imaginary the global imaginary of a society could be applied, with the appropriate adaptations, to other historical periods and improve their understanding. It could also be used to better refine the reading of a society at a given time, sorting out and then confronting the imaginary of different groups—as these different tribes that today are to be seen on the social field.

If, after an initial reservation, the clothing imaginary is to be regarded as a privileged means to access the underground currents of a society, some practical applications can spark contrasted reactions. One can hesitate, indeed, to adhere to a perspective that considers too systematically that the success of designers comes from the coincidence of their personal clothing imaginary and the general clothing imaginary of a period. On the contrary, one can be tempted, not only to accept it, but to draw from this perspective some commercial implications and utilize it as a marketing device. One way or the other, it would be failing to recognize the free character of the act of creation. We should be aware that in the coincidence mentioned above, there is no mechanical relation, but a random encounter between a work grounded on personal components and the spirit of the time, determined by multiple and complex elements. While an individual creation never deliberately coincides with the creation of a specific period, a strong individual creation can very well, as it has been underlined in this essay, significantly direct, as far as clothes are concerned, a collective imaginary. And, when one knows the important part that clothes have in modifying representations and behaviors, one may dream the new century would be back to seduction and elegance and would drive fashion and the world out of the reluctance and moral shrinking in which they stand.

Even if the social function of clothing could be somewhat limited by these remarks, it remains, like its heuristic function, very strong. If we were to underestimate it, we would lose a very valuable tool for understanding contemporary societies and, at the same time, an indispensable basis for other anthropological, economic, and psychological studies. On this basis, we can rethink the relationships we have with clothing on an individual level —without mentioning pathologies. Incidentally, it may be because this foundation was missing that a psychoanalysis of clothing, which Henry Flügel initiated in 1930 with *The Psychology of Clothing*, has not yet found a way to develop. If this essay could contribute to this, it would, of course, not have been useless. But he was even more ambitious. Playing on the dialectic between the frivolity that weighs on clothes and the depth that I have returned to it, he had the ambition to affirm their fleetingness and, consequently, to make of this joyful lightness and depth of being that they imply in themselves, as in the discourse that they inspire, the ultimate model of an ethics of life and thought.

INDEX

Campbell N., 119
Cardin P., 45, 46, 61, 62, 63, 79, 111, 135, 159
Carlyle Th., 23
Carné M., 161
Catroux B., 139
Chalayan H., 121
Chanel, 41, 42, 44, 47, 50, 63, 83, 95, 138
Coblence F., 31
Cocteau J., 145
Courrèges A., 37, 46, 47, 58, 69, 71, 86, 111, 135
Crawford C., 119

Delacroix, 63, 66
Delcourt M., 147
Dessès J., 50
Dior Ch., 50, 59, 63, 117, 132, 136, 140, 146
Dumont L., 27, 140
Durand G., 9, 10, 17, 22, 23, 51, 101, 102, 104, 105,
    115, 122, 123, 126, 141, 148, 167

Elbaz A., 149
Eliade M., 51, 147
Elias N., 14
Esterel J., 79
Evangelista L., 119

www.ingramcontent.com/pod-product-compliance
Lightning Source LLC
Chambersburg PA
CBHW070515160726
48003CB00004B/1580